SpringerBriefs in Computer Science

SpringerBriefs present concise summaries of cutting-edge research and practical applications across a wide spectrum of fields. Featuring compact volumes of 50 to 125 pages, the series covers a range of content from professional to academic.

Typical topics might include:

- A timely report of state-of-the art analytical techniques
- A bridge between new research results, as published in journal articles, and a contextual literature review
- A snapshot of a hot or emerging topic
- An in-depth case study or clinical example
- A presentation of core concepts that students must understand in order to make independent contributions

Briefs allow authors to present their ideas and readers to absorb them with minimal time investment. Briefs will be published as part of Springer's eBook collection, with millions of users worldwide. In addition, Briefs will be available for individual print and electronic purchase. Briefs are characterized by fast, global electronic dissemination, standard publishing contracts, easy-to-use manuscript preparation and formatting guidelines, and expedited production schedules. We aim for publication 8–12 weeks after acceptance. Both solicited and unsolicited manuscripts are considered for publication in this series.

More information about this series at http://www.springer.com/series/10028

Gaurav Baranwal · Dinesh Kumar
Zahid Raza · Deo Prakash Vidyarthi

Auction Based Resource Provisioning in Cloud Computing

 Springer

Gaurav Baranwal
Department of Computer Science
Institute of Science, Banaras Hindu
  University
Varanasi, Uttar Pradesh, India

Dinesh Kumar
School of Computer and Systems Sciences
Jawaharlal Nehru University
New Delhi, India

Zahid Raza
School of Computer and Systems Sciences
Jawaharlal Nehru University
New Delhi, India

Deo Prakash Vidyarthi
School of Computer and Systems Sciences
Jawaharlal Nehru University
New Delhi, India

ISSN 2191-5768   ISSN 2191-5776 (electronic)
SpringerBriefs in Computer Science
ISBN 978-981-10-8736-3   ISBN 978-981-10-8737-0 (eBook)
https://doi.org/10.1007/978-981-10-8737-0

Library of Congress Control Number: 2018944359

Printed on acid-free paper

This Springer imprint is published by the registered company Springer Nature Singapore Pte Ltd.
The registered company address is: 152 Beach Road, #21-01/04 Gateway East, Singapore 189721, Singapore

Dedicated to
All who are contributing in the just allocation
of the resources

Foreword

It gives me a pleasure to write a foreword for this book and gives me an honour to congratulate the authors of this book for a job well done. This is a timely presentation, and the scope of the topics covered in the book provides the reader with up-to-the-moment resources in the area of Cloud resource provisioning.

Cloud computing, a business model of computing, has revolutionized the world by its enormous benefits. Cloud computing resources such as CPU, memory, storage, network are available on demand, and anyone can avail these services on a subscription basis. Cloud computing is a business model of computing unlike grid and cluster, so pricing of the Cloud resources can act as a lever to control the wastage of the computing resources. At present, most of the Cloud services are being offered using static pricing. The drawback with static pricing is its non-compliance of demand and supply principle of economics resulting in an inefficient control of the utilization of computing resources. Dynamic pricing is obviously a better solution for this problem.

Amazon proved that auction results in the efficient allocation of resources compared to static pricing. It is beneficial to both Cloud providers and Cloud customers. But, to my best knowledge, besides Amazon, no provider is offering resources using auction mechanism. This area needs proper attention from professionals and academicians to identify the suitable reasons for this and offer remedies. Recently, Google took a step forward and started offering virtual machines using dynamic pricing on a trial basis. I have proposed resource provisioning models that apply auction. Professor Vidyarthi is also an active researcher and with his group members has proposed a good number of models that apply auction. What is lacking is an organized literature that motivates researchers in the field of Cloud computing to contribute in this area further.

This book introduces auction mechanism for resource provisioning in Cloud computing. The aim of this book is to provide a structured literature of auction based on Cloud market to attract academicians and professionals to contribute in this area. Since various models have also been proposed, it will help readers to formulate the Cloud resource allocation problem using auction. This book also discusses challenges in detail, and the reader will be able to understand them.

In fact, various ingredients of auction-based Cloud market have been combined at one place.

It is to emphasize that auction-based Cloud market needs expertise from both computer scientists and economists. It provides a good opportunity for interdisciplinary research. The developed services must reach the society; otherwise, it would be a failure. This book will act as a bridge between computer scientists with specialization in Cloud computing and economists with specialization in resource allocation using auction.

Melbourne, Australia   Dr. Rajkumar Buyya
                                   Redmond Barry Distinguished Professor
                                    Director, Cloud Computing and Distributed
                                   Systems (CLOUDS) Lab, School of Computing
                                               and Information Systems
                                              The University of Melbourne

Preface

Cloud computing, a business model of computing, has revolutionized the world by its enormous benefits. Computing resources such as CPU, memory, storage are available in the form of services online, and one can avail these services on payment. In 2006, Amazon launched various types of Cloud services and named it Elastic Compute Cloud (EC2). This step accelerated the well acceptance of the Cloud services and established a whole new market of the computing resources. A good number of service providers joined the Cloud bandwagon and started offering various types of Cloud services in order to attract the customers. Of all the early service providers, a common attribute was the pricing of these services as it was based on the principle of static pricing. Various services were available in the Cloud, but at fixed rates. These service providers increased their infrastructure to cater more number of Cloud customers. A common problem, encountered by most of these providers, was less number of requests at off-peak period which kept most of the infrastructure idle. Though virtualization is the main ingredient for creating Cloud services in order to best utilize the resources, even to run virtual machines of low power a physical machine with substantive power is needed. Various professionals argued that scheduling policies can be designed to handle the challenge of wastage of computing resources, but it was observed that scheduling alone would not suffice. Unlike grid and cluster, an important characteristic of Cloud computing is its business model of computing in which pricing of the resources acts as a lever to control the wastage of the computing resources. Thus, the main drawback with static pricing was its non-adherence to the demand and supply principle of economics, making it difficult to control the better utilization of the computing resources. Dynamic pricing is naturally a better option for the pricing of such resources.

Although researchers across have suggested various approaches to implement dynamic pricing, perhaps industries are not ready to accept so. It is because of the ease of static pricing; it is very simple in nature and more understandable to the customers. In 2009, Amazon took a bold step and launched a type of instance (i.e. virtual machine) which would be available using spot mechanism, a type of auction. Cloud customers were smart enough to understand this, as reduction in price is a motivating factor. Since then, Amazon has created a glorious history of spot instances (read on Amazon EC2 on huge reduction in price paid by Cloud customers using spot instances). The crucial issue with spot instance, which makes it more reasonable and cheaper for Cloud customer, is non-guarantee of resources as Amazon may take back the allocated spot instances whenever there is a shortfall of the resources assigned using static pricing. This issue warrants smartness from the customers in terms of fault tolerance schemes.

Amazon proved that auction has the ability of effective allocation of resources as compared to static pricing. It is beneficial to both Cloud providers and Cloud customers. Unfortunately, except Amazon to our best knowledge, no other provider offers the Cloud resources using auction mechanism. Therefore, proper attention is warranted from the Cloud professionals and academicians to identify the appropriate reasons for this and suggest best remedies for the promotion of applying auction for the Cloud resources. Recently, Google started offering pre-emptive virtual machines similar to Amazon spot instances, though on a trial basis.

While making a survey on resource allocation, using auction in Cloud computing, it is observed that very few researchers have contributed significantly in this area of research. What majorly lacks is well-organized structured literature that can motivate the researchers, working in the area of Cloud computing for more significant contribution.

This book is intended to offer an organized literature that deliberates on auction mechanism for resource provisioning and pricing in Cloud computing. Chapter 1 introduces the fundamental knowledge of Cloud computing that will help naïve in the field of Cloud computing to cultivate sufficient background for understanding Cloud computing, Cloud market, and how pricing acts as a lever, i.e. how economical approaches can be applied for the allocation of computing resources and most importantly why auction is significant in Cloud computing. Chapter 2 provides a comprehensive study of auction, available in the literature, and describes its various types to be applied in the different market scenarios. As literature reports only few types of auction in Cloud computing, this chapter generates sufficient motivation to identify different Cloud market scenarios in which various types of auction can be used. First two chapters are the prerequisites for those readers who are novice in Cloud computing and therefore may be skipped by those equipped with sufficient background in Cloud and auction. Auction has generally been categorized into three classes based on the role of customer and provider: forward auction, reverse auction and double auction. A detailed description of forward auction in Cloud computing has been provided in Chap. 3, of reverse auction in Chap. 4 and of double auction in Chap. 5. These three Chaps. 3, 4 and 5, discuss the advantages and disadvantages of the corresponding auction types along with the detailed framework and a model that provides sufficient background to the researchers in order to understand and formulate resource allocation problem using auction under various Cloud market scenarios. Chapters 3, 4 and 5 also enlist open research issues to be considered as a potential research problem for the researchers. Chapter 6 summarizes and concludes this brief.

Varanasi, India   Gaurav Baranwal
New Delhi, India   Dinesh Kumar
New Delhi, India   Zahid Raza
New Delhi, India   Deo Prakash Vidyarthi

Contents

About the Authors

Gaurav Baranwal is an assistant professor at the Department of Computer Science, Institute of Science, Banaras Hindu University, Varanasi, UP, India. Before, he served as an assistant professor in Madan Mohan Malviya University of Technology, Gorakhpur, India. He completed his M.Tech. and Ph.D. in computer science from the School of Computer and Systems Sciences, Jawaharlal Nehru University, New Delhi, India. His research interests include resource provisioning and service coordination in Cloud computing.

Dinesh Kumar is a Ph.D. student at the School of Computer and Systems Sciences, Jawaharlal Nehru University, New Delhi, India. He completed his M.Tech. in Computer Science at the School of Computer and Systems Sciences, Jawaharlal Nehru University, New Delhi, India. His research interests include resource provisioning and pricing in Cloud computing.

Zahid Raza is an associate professor at the School of Computer and Systems Sciences, Jawaharlal Nehru University (JNU), New Delhi, India. He received his Ph.D. in computer science from Jawaharlal Nehru University, New Delhi, India. Prior to joining JNU, he served at Banasthali Vidyapith University, Rajasthan, India. His research interests include parallel and distributed systems, evolutionary algorithms, Cloud computing and IoT.

Deo Prakash Vidyarthi is a professor at the School of Computer and Systems Sciences, Jawaharlal Nehru University, New Delhi. He has published over 90 research papers in various peer-reviewed international journals and transactions (including IEEE, Elsevier, Springer, Wiley, World Scientific) and over 50 research papers in the proceedings of various conferences in India and abroad. He has also contributed many chapters in related disciplines. He has two research monographs to his credit and has also contributed chapters in many edited books. He serves on the editorial boards of many international journals and is a senior member of IEEE;

International Association of Computer Science and Information Technology (IACSIT), Singapore; International Society of Research in Science and Technology (ISRST), USA; and International Association of Engineers (IAENG). His research interests include parallel and distributed systems, grid and Cloud computing, mobile computing and evolutionary computing.

Acronyms

BB	Budget-balance
BO	Bidder's optimality
C-BIC	Cloud-bayesian incentive compatible
C-DSIC	Cloud-dominant strategy incentive compatible
C-OPT	Cloud-optimal
CA	Combinatorial auction
CCIF	Cloud computing interoperability forum
CDA	Continuous double auction
CDARA	Combinatorial double auction resource allocation
CFP	Call for proposal
CMO	Cell membrane optimization
CRC	Cloud resource consumer
CRP	Cloud resource provider
DMAA	Double multi-attribute auction
EE	Economic efficiency
FCC	Federal communications commission
FMCDAM	Fair multi-attribute combinatorial double auction model
GVA	Generalized vickrey auction
IaaS	Infrastructure as a service
IC	Incentive compatible
ICT	Information and communication technologies
IDC	International data corporation
ILP	Integer linear programming
IR	Individual rationality
JADE	Java agent development framework
LP	Linear programming
MA	Multi-attribute
MIP	Mixed-integer programming
MVA	Modified vickrey auction
MVO	Mean variance optimization

ND	Non-dominance
NIST	National institute of standards and technology
OVF	Open virtualization format
PaaS	Platform as a service
PFA	Paddy field algorithm
PIP	Packing integer programming
PMDA	Preston-mcAfee double auction
PTAS	Polynomial time approximation scheme
QoS	Quality of service
RBMA	Reverse batch making auction
SaaS	Software as a service
SAA	Simultaneously ascending auction
SLA	Service-level agreement
SME	Small and medium enterprises
SVM	Support vector machine
SW	Social welfare
TCRA	Truthful combinatorial reverse auction
TDACC	Truthful multi-unit double auction for cloud computing
TPDA	Threshold price double auction
VCG	Vickrey–clarke–groves
VM	Virtual machine
VMPAC	VM provisioning and allocation problem for cloud computing
WDP	Winner determination problem

Chapter 1
Introduction

Abstract Cloud computing has evolved through various phases from distributed computing, mobile computing, grid computing and currently is in most evolved form of the computing. Cloud computing is basically a business model where various hardware resources such as CPU, network, storage and software resources such as platform, applications are available on demand and are offered as utility; i.e., a Cloud user has to pay for the usage of the Cloud resources. The proliferation of the Internet has made possible the availability of the Cloud services across the globe, though private Cloud exists on intranet. As Cloud is a business model, a large number of players have joined the Cloud platform with their services. Recently, a tough competition has been noticed in the Cloud market for the offered services as both the number of providers and customers have increased to a large extent. Though it creates a good opportunity for both provider and customer, it also results in a number of issues to be addressed properly to make the Cloud market more beneficial for the customer and the provider. This chapter takes a look at widely accepted Cloud computing definitions, explains its concepts and summarizes various services and deployment models of Cloud computing. This chapter also gives an overview of benefits and challenges of the Cloud computing. Further, it describes pricing in detail to understand the need for auction of the Cloud resources followed by a mention on the organization of the book. The aim of this chapter is to offer a prerequisite to understand the concepts discussed further in the book and its role in research.

1.1 Cloud Computing

Cloud computing has become an integral part of the modern life. Most of the Internet of things (IoTs) devices use Cloud services, knowingly or unknowingly, making IoT and Cloud computing inseparable. Cloud computing is a new paradigm for utility computing, is growing very rapidly and is attracting the attention of not only the big business organizations but also of research and academia, government, small and medium enterprises, etc.

© The Author(s) 2018

G. Baranwal et al., *Auction Based Resource Provisioning in Cloud Computing*,
SpringerBriefs in Computer Science, https://doi.org/10.1007/978-981-10-8737-0_1

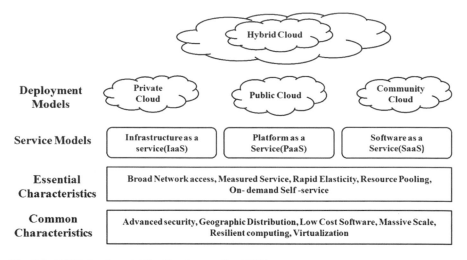

Fig. 1.1 NIST visual model for Cloud computing [110]

Depending upon its role and functionality, Cloud computing has been defined in differential manners covering its different aspects by the various organizations. NIST (National Institute of Standards and Technology) defines the Cloud computing as *"Cloud computing is a model for enabling ubiquitous, convenient, on-demand network access to a shared pool of configurable computing resources (e.g. networks, servers, storage, applications, and services) that can be rapidly provisioned and released with minimal managerial effort or service provider interaction"* [110]. Figure 1.1 shows the NIST visual model for Cloud computing.

A report from European Union provides definition of Cloud as *"an elastic execution environment of resources involving multiple stakeholders and providing a metered service at multiple granularities for a specified level of quality (of service)"* [166].

Since Cloud computing is an evolution from parallel and distributed computing, grid and mobile computing, it includes commercialization as well as the virtualization technology. Thus, a broadly accepted definition of Cloud given by Buyya [32] is *"Cloud is a type of parallel and distributed system consisting of collection of inter-connected and virtualized computers that are dynamically provisioned and presented as one or more unified computing resources based on service-level agreements established through negotiation between the service provider and consumers"*.

As Cloud has been evolved from distributed and grid computing, it inherits the features of distributed and grid computing. Significant improvement in distributed and grid computing, over the time, has made the Cloud computing more interesting. Thus, analysing various features of Cloud computing, it can be described as follows: *"Cloud is a pool of virtualized computing resources (e.g. CPU, memory, storage, software etc.), automatically and dynamically provisioned to customers on pay-per-use basis supporting elasticity, workload migration, metering etc"*. From various definitions of Cloud, the main characteristics of the Cloud computing inferred are on-demand, measured and metered service, multi-tenant, elasticity, easy-to-use, etc.

Some popular examples of emerging Cloud computing infrastructure/platform are Microsoft Azure, Amazon EC2, GoogleApp Engine, VMWare and Aneka.

1.1.1   Essential Characteristics of Cloud

The essential features/characteristics of the Cloud are listed as follows [172].

On-demand Self-service

Least human intervention is needed for the resource provisioning. Resources such as CPU cycle, storage can be provisioned unilaterally by the consumer automatically.

Broad Network Access

If a user has some heterogeneous thin or thick client platforms such as laptops, mobiles and Internet connection, the user can access the services of Cloud from anywhere and at anytime.

Resource Pooling

Multi-tenant model is used to pool the computing resources for serving multiple consumers. Various physical and virtual resources can be dynamically assigned and reassigned as per the consumer's need. Users, generally, are not aware of the exact location of the resources offered though at the higher level of abstraction like data centre, state, country, a user may specify the location of the offered resources. Examples of resources are virtual machine, CPU cycle, memory and network bandwidth.

Rapid Elasticity

In Cloud, resources can be provisioned rapidly and elastically; i.e., it can quickly be added up and rapidly released to quickly scale down. Cloud resources are visualized as unlimited, so consumers can purchase them in any desired quantity at any time.

Measured Service

Cloud adds metering capability to control and optimize its resources. Transparency is provided by monitoring, controlling and reporting of the resource usage for both the provider and customer of the utilized services.

1.1.2   Cloud Service Models

Cloud computing provides hardware/software resources on a subscription basis in a pay-as-you-go model to its consumers. Broadly, these Cloud services are categorized as software as a service (SaaS), platform as a service (PaaS) and infrastructure as a service (IaaS). Services are not confined to only these models and can be extended as well. The types of Cloud service models are as follows.

Software as a Service (SaaS)

It is a model in which applications not necessarily are to be installed and run on the user's own computer. It relieves the users from the burden of the software maintenance and support. Thin client interfaces (e.g. Web browser) are sufficient to access the applications. Expensive licenses, for all the software, need not to be purchased. Limitations for user-specific application configuration settings are only one exception in this. Major players in SaaS are Google App Engine, Facebook, YouTube, Salesforce.com, etc.

Platform as a Service (PaaS)

It is a model that offers a platform, to the Cloud users, to develop their applications. The platform consists of programming languages and software tools supported by the service provider. Underlying Cloud infrastructure such as operating systems, servers, networks, storage is not managed by the user. Only the deployed applications and application hosting environment are managed by the user. Major players offering PaaS are Google App Engine, Microsoft Azure, Amazon Simple DB, etc.

Infrastructure as a Service (IaaS)

A model in which users outsource the computing resources, i.e. hardware as well as other infrastructure in the form of virtual machines to support their applications. Users can deploy and run their applications with outsourced resources. The IaaS provider owns the computing resources and is responsible for housing, running and maintaining them. User typically pays for the resources on a per-use basis. Underlying Cloud infrastructure is not managed by the user, but they have control over operating systems, servers, storage, deployed applications and possibly networking components. IaaS allows users to avoid the large capital expenses with infrastructure and data centres. Major players, offering IaaS, are GoGrid, Amazon EC2, FlexiScale, etc.

Figure 1.2 shows the various service models of Cloud computing. The importance of these service models can be understood by a report from the University of Berkeley [10] "*Cloud computing, the long-held dream of computing as a utility, has the potential to transform a large part of the IT industry making software even more attractive as a service*".

Fig. 1.2 Cloud service
models

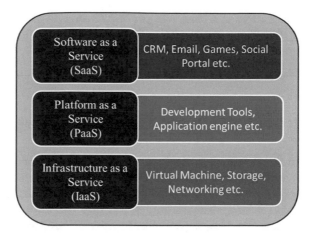

1.1.3 Deployment Models

IBM made a classification of the Cloud based on its architecture which is as follows.

Private Cloud

A private Cloud is rented or owned by an organization. The whole private Cloud resources are used by that organization to serve its private purposes. For example, an enterprise built a Cloud to serve its business's critical applications. RackSpace, IBM CloudPrivate and VMware are the key players to deploy private Cloud.

Community Cloud

A private Cloud is called a community Cloud, when Cloud resources support a community with similar interests and are shared by several organizations. Either a third party manages such Cloud or participating organizations control and operate it in a collaborative fashion. GoogleApps for Government and Microsoft Government community Cloud are examples of community Cloud.

Public Cloud

The Cloud infrastructure is owned by a service provider, and Cloud resources are made available to the general public or a large industry on a rental basis. Users rent the resources and can scale up or down in response to load variation in its application. Microsoft Azure, Amazon EC2 and Google Cloud Platform are major key players in public Cloud market.

Hybrid Cloud

A hybrid Cloud is the combination of two or more Cloud types—private, community or public Cloud. In case of high demand or some specific services, a private Cloud may hire the services of a public Cloud. This creates a hybrid Cloud. If the user is using a hybrid Cloud, it is possible to migrate some computing resources from a private Cloud to the public Cloud. Software layer such as Eucalyptus can act as a bridge between private Cloud and public Cloud. vCloud is an offering of VMWARE to deploy hybrid Cloud.

1.1.4 Major Benefits of Cloud Computing

In recent years, leading IT enterprises, e.g. Amazon, Google, Microsoft, have promoted the Cloud for better utilization of their under-utilized computing resources. It liberates the small and medium enterprises (SMEs) from investing the capital on infrastructure, maintenance, etc., as they can avail these Cloud services from the vendors. Besides, various other benefits of Cloud and promotion of Cloud by big IT enterprises in recent years have attracted the attention of customers. Though there are enormous benefits of Cloud computing, some major such benefits are listed as follows.

Cost Effective

In traditional computing, user has to buy the equipment and has to pay for its operational expenditure. Operational cost increases with the increase in the user base. In Cloud computing, user's jobs are outsourced to data centres. A user needs to pay only the operational cost. Cloud computing will reduce computing costs significantly for both; small users and organizations. According to IDC (International Data Corporation), *"IDC expects that enterprises that do not improve their automation capabilities, whether through Cloud computing or otherwise, will see their IT costs continue to rise significantly"* [14].

Scalability and Elasticity

Upon the growth of a business, more computing resources are warranted. Cloud computing may help here. It is not required to buy, install and configure new hardware or software; rather, resources can be pooled from the Cloud service providers on a rental basis. On the completion of the job, these hired resources may be returned back to the Cloud. One does not have to pay for the unwanted resources.

Agility

"Cloud Computing is a model for provisioning and consuming IT capabilities on a need and pay-per-use basis. This helps in shifting the cost structure from capital expenditure to operating expenditure and helps the IT systems become more agile" [182]. Resources can be provisioned quickly on the requirement. Hence, there will be more time to devour business market.

Device and Location Independence

One can access the Cloud services from anywhere and at any time through the Internet. Cloud services can be accessed through Desktop, PDAs or a smartphone. Thus, Cloud services are device- and location-independent.

Multi-tenancy

In Cloud computing, multiple users can access the single and same application, though they have access only to their own data.

Low Energy Consumption

According to a study released by Accenture, Microsoft and WSP Environment & Energy, it is observed that carbon emission and energy consumption can be reduced by 30% or more, if large organizations move their business applications to Cloud. This study also finds that small businesses get benefited by garnering substantially higher savings [3]. Outsourcing via Cloud computing enables a Cloud consumer to become more environment-friendly.

1.1.5 Cloud Challenges

Cloud computing is in its infancy. Day by day, the number of Cloud customers is increasing and so are Cloud service providers. Since in Cloud computing, consumers put their data and run their application at someone else's resources, one of the most important concerns is the consideration of privacy. There are many other important research issues and challenges that need to be addressed. Some key issues like resource provisioning, security, interoperability, standardization, SLA require a deeper and conscious addressing in order for Cloud to be fully functional [157].

Cost Model

Authors in [52] pointed out that the Cloud consumers must consider the trade-off among computation, integration and communication. In traditional computing, user has to pay for the equipment, operational expenditure and maintenance of the computer system including personnel and service cost. Cloud computing is pay-per-use model, so the user has to pay for the operational cost. The usage of Cloud services decreases infrastructure cost, but it does raise the data communication cost. A consumer can use the services of more than one Cloud provider, so it also adds the integration cost. Complication in cost analysis is made by elastic resource pooling and multi-tenancy.

Service-Level Agreement (SLA)

"Although Cloud consumers do not have control over the underlying computing resources (in case of SaaS/PaaS user), they do need to ensure of the quality, availability, reliability, and performance of these resources when consumers have migrated their core business functions onto their entrusted Cloud. In other words, it is vital for the consumers to obtain guarantees from service providers on service delivery. Typically, these are provided through Service Level Agreements (SLAs) negotiated between the providers and consumers" [52]. SLA is a bilateral agreement; the conditions and constraints of a given service are stated, and the agreed QoS is also characterized between the provider and the customer using a set of metric. The general objective of a service provider is to maximize its profit and customer satisfaction. In cost model challenge, different types of costs involved in Cloud computing are already mentioned. It also includes the penalty cost. Penalty cost provides risk transfer for the consumer, when agreement is violated by the provider. There are continuing changes in operations and operating environment, so change in QoS is also to be done over the time. With the increasing demand and unpredictable workload of Cloud computing, providers are facing the problem of meeting SLA claims.

Cloud Scalability, Interoperability and Standardization

As Cloud computing uses pay-as-you-go model, consumers/users desire to scale quickly up and down with load variation in their applications in order to save money. In this situation, it is difficult to maintain SLA for the vendor.

At present, each Cloud provider has its own way on interaction of Cloud customer or applications with the Cloud. It creates two problems. First, optimization of resource usage at different levels is required which creates difficulty for consumers in choosing the vendors. Second, organizations have their own legacy system whose integration with Cloud is a difficult task. Interoperability is required in order to overcome the above problems.

For load balancing and resource usage optimization, live migration is required. It needs a heterogeneous hardware platform hypervisor to run virtual machines. So a uniform standard must be maintained by the providers.

Resource Provisioning

Cloud consumers hire computing resources from different vendors to execute their applications (jobs). Before execution of a job, vendor provisions the resources. Dynamism is an important characteristic of Cloud computing and resource requirement can be scaled up and down according to the consumer's requirements. Job is constrained by finishing time, budget and SLA. Service providers need some resource provisioning method for optimal resource utilization which is a challenging task. Resource provisioning mechanism also has to satisfy certain constraints such as time limit, resource budget, QoS maximization depending on the application. To do this, there is a need of fast and effective decision models and optimization algorithms for the resource manager. The difficulty in efficient resource provisioning comes from unpredictable demand, hardware and software failures, and conflicts in SLA.

Security

Cloud consumers face some security threats both from inside and outside of the Cloud. Multi-tenancy and resource pooling in Cloud have created newer security threats. The robust and fool proof techniques are needed to handle such security threats.

Legal and Regulatory Issues

The presence of geographically distributed Cloud consumers and service providers creates new legal challenges. If Cloud consumers and providers are functional at different places of the globe, they are subject to numerous regulatory requirements.

1.2 Pricing of Cloud Resources

Cloud service providers offer various types of services to its customers. Customers vie for maximum QoS at minimum pricing. Customer-friendly pricing schemes can attract a good number of customers, but, ultimately, the goal of the provider is revenue maximization. Thus, it is required to design optimal pricing schemes to satisfy both—customers and providers. Provisioning the resources to make Cloud providers and Cloud customers benefit in terms of cost, QoS, etc., is a challenging task. Single-pricing scheme cannot be optimal in all the scenarios; e.g., a provider can offer resources comparatively at low price when customer avails those resources for a longer period of time. Similarly, provider can charge comparatively higher price if customer wants resources on demand. Offering a pricing scheme that considers important factors such as resource type, QoS can encourage the customer to use the Cloud services.

As Cloud computing is a business model of computing, the pricing of computing resources acts as a lever in controlling the provisioning of the resources. Recent development in Cloud computing has forced the Cloud providers to nudge the pricing schemes. Due to growing popularity of the Cloud computing, various service providers such as Amazon, Google, IBM, Oracle have started offering Cloud services with varying pricing schemes. There is a stiff competition in the Cloud market and various attractive offerings are available. Therefore, service providers conceive various scenarios in Cloud where different pricing schemes may be applied. Professionals need to understand the real market conditions such as interest of customer, competition in market, utilization of resources to decide on the pricing schemes. Researchers need to design various pricing models appropriate for a particular scenario.

To develop a suitable pricing model in Cloud is a complex job because of rapidly changing Cloud market scenario. Competition in the Cloud market has increased, attractive offers are available from the providers, and inter-Cloud is reducing vendor-lock in problem. For example, Amazon offers three types of VM instances called reserved instance, on-demand instance and spot instance. In reserved and on-demand instances, all the customers have to pay the same fixed price per unit of time, while price of spot instances depends on the market condition.

Professionals need to understand various schemes, proposed in the literature, to adopt them in a real world. A discussion on pros and cons of various pricing schemes is warranted. An agreement, between service provider and customer for the business of resources, uses a particular pricing model. Generally, modelling of resource provisioning in Cloud is done either by convention or by applying some economic approaches. In conventional approaches, all participants are assumed to be non-strategic, and at the same time, they do not consider competition and behaviour of the market. While in economic approaches, participants, called agents, are considered as rational and strategic. In decision-making, competition and market behaviour are also considered during modelling of dynamic pricing. Since both Cloud customer and Cloud provider are intelligent and self-interested in the Cloud market, economic approaches are more suitable as compared to conventional ones.

The pricing schemes in the Cloud can be classified into two: static pricing and dynamic pricing. Reserved instances and on-demand instances are offered under static pricing scheme, while spot instances are offered under dynamic pricing scheme. Both static and dynamic pricing schemes are discussed, in detail, as follows.

1.2.1 Static Pricing

In static pricing schemes, Cloud providers can offer two types of provisioning plans for the computing resources—pre-decided (reservation) and on-demand [38].

1.2.1.1 Pre-decided (Reservation) Plan

In reservation plan, Cloud customer requests for the Cloud resources for a longer duration from the Cloud service providers and pays one-time cost, e.g. one year contract of certain Cloud resources. As the prices are fixed throughout the contract, it is also known as static or fixed policy through customer's requirements that need to be pre-decided. Armbrust et al. [10] describe three possible cases of reservation plan which are shown in Fig. 1.3. In case 1, i.e. Fig. 1.3a, if a customer reserves the resources required at peak time (shown by capacity line) for a longer period, the customer suffers the loss (i.e. shaded area shows heavy resource wastage). In case 2, i.e. Figure 1.3b, if customer reserves less than required resources at peak time, both customer and provider suffer the loss (i.e. waste of resources still exist when demand is less than reserved resources and demand by the customer is not fulfilled when

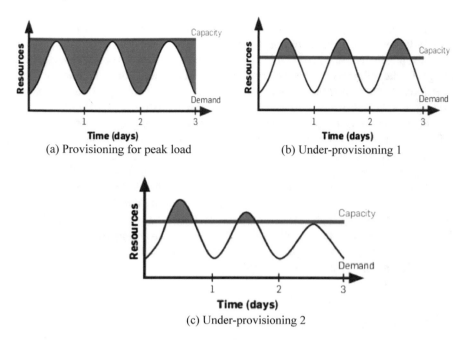

Fig. 1.3 Three cases of Cloud resource provisioning without elasticity [10]

demand is greater than reserved resources.) In third case, i.e. Fig. 1.3c, when demand decreases with time, user faces more resource wastage. To prevent this resource waste, Cloud customer may give up those services which may not be beneficial for both customer and provider. Reservation plan faces this situation because of unpredictability or fluctuations in customer's demand. In under-provisioning and over-provisioning, both the customer and the provider suffer.

1.2.1.2   On-demand Plan

In on-demand plan, the problems of pre-decided plan can be removed. If there is under-provisioning, one can pool more resources on demand though at the cost of increased price. In case of over-provisioning, on-demand plan can use some mechanism for better utilization of resources.

On-demand plan follows pay-per-use policy. This makes it suitable for unpredictable or fluctuating demand. In reservation plan, Cloud user pays for one month or one year for the services of Cloud before the utilization of computing resources. In the reservation plan, a Cloud user has to pay less in comparison with on-demand plan, because user reserves the computing resources for a longer duration as compared to an on-demand plan [38]. According to [5], reservation plan can save provisioning cost up to 49% if resources are fully utilized.

Fixed pricing is more predictable and stable. Customer is able to decide concrete budget for the utilization of the resources and does not need to bother the sudden surge in market. Though, there is a risk of paying more, if one would pay using dynamic pricing. If value of resource in the market increases, customer gets the benefit and provider suffers loss. It can be understood by a simple example; suppose a provider offers its computing resources and fixes the price of these computing resources for its use/rent. At any time, these resources may be over-utilized or under-utilized but since the prices for the resources are fixed, it may affect the utilization of the resource which in turn may affect the revenue of the provider. While in case of decrement in value of resource in the market, providers get benefits but the customer would suffer loss by paying high. Therefore, fixed price can be a benefit or a detriment. Dynamic pricing got attention of both, researchers and professionals, because of the drawbacks static pricing carries. It includes inflexibility, difficulty in formation of equilibrium price and less economical [209].

1.2.2 Dynamic Pricing

Dynamic pricing allows a provider to decide the price of the resources on the basis of demand and supply of the resources in the market. Providers enjoy a potential profit with dynamic pricing. Low price of the resource does not necessarily mean provider would suffer a loss. Low pricing is often done to attract more customers which in turn may increase the revenue of the providers. Dynamic pricing not only increases the utilization of the resources, which is beneficial for both Cloud service provider and Cloud user, but also improves competition in the Cloud market i.e. provider is able to maximize its revenue even with excess capacity of resources and customer is able to avail the services with minimum pricing [113]. Dynamic pricing generally offers real-time data related to business about current market conditions. Using this data, providers can evaluate the effectiveness of their market strategy. This data also helps customers to understand the market condition to design their strategy in the market. For example, Amazon EC2 provides on-demand instances and reserved instances with associated prices that come under fixed pricing scheme. In addition, it also provides spot pricing instances under dynamic pricing scheme. Amazon introduced the spot market, where customer can rent unused computing instances at very low price. In spot pricing (an auction mechanism), user needs to bid maximum price that the user is willing to pay for renting the unused computing instances. Meanwhile, if market price (bid) for the rented resource becomes more than user's bid, resources will be terminated instantly from the current user. Amazon EC2 provides Spot instance price history for last 90 days which can be collected from Amazon EC2 API tool [4]. Based on this history, users can decide the bids. Though Amazon states that spot price varies based on real demand and supply of the spot instances, but current pattern of pricing may not occur in future, i.e. historical trends do not guarantee the future results.

1.3   Need of Auction in Cloud

To decide the value of a computing resource, for a customer by the provider, is very difficult. Same applies to a Cloud customer, i.e. to make the right payment of a particular resource. Though dynamic pricing has various benefits, it creates difficulty to the providers on deciding the price of its services. Even customers face difficulty to decide the exact budget for the required resources. Another issue in Cloud, that needs proper attention, is utilization of spare resources which can be resolved by proper dynamic pricing. Resources in Cloud are perishable in nature, e.g. CPU cycle, memory, network bandwidth cannot be preserved for future sale. If a virtual machine is created and not allocated, it is the wastage of the resources of a data centre. Similarly, if a virtual machine is created on a physical machine; entire physical machine and not a part of it is at stake. At the provider side, a large number of spare resources should be allocated to the customers to best utilize the resources. At the same time, customers are attracted to utilize these spare resources because of its low cost. This results in the increasing revenue of the provider.

Various methods such as auction, bargaining, negotiation have been used to implement the concept of dynamic pricing. But auction can be a real bet for dynamic pricing that may overcome the above-mentioned difficulties of dynamic pricing. Auction is quite effective to address the market competition and allows participants to decide on the price of the services. Auction is used in the market environment where the goods or objects have no standard values and the pricing is based on the supply and demand principle. In auction, there are three main entities; buyer, seller and auctioneer. Buyer pays the money and purchases the resources, seller offers the resources and earns the revenue while auctioneer conducts and controls the auction.

In auction, the pricing of the resources is decided by the bidders and since bidders are the competitors, winning bidders praise themselves in order to win while losers blame other participating bidders. In Cloud computing, auction is a quite effective technique to remove the drawbacks of both static and dynamic pricing. Mechanism design, a sub-field of the game theory, helps to design auction to deal strategic and intelligent participants in the market. It is an appropriate economic mechanism for the allocation of the resources and pricing in Cloud computing.

1.4   Organization of the Book

This book contains six chapters. Chapters are structured in a way to prevail the interest of the readers till the end. Before starting the discussion on challenges and possible solutions, a sufficient background has been provided so that both naïve as well as the experienced researchers get sufficient motivation. Therefore, the domain of Cloud computing and auction have been prompted first. Further chapters are organized on the basis of types of auction to furnish a whole view of auction in Cloud computing. Though, various categorization of auction is possible, in literature auction is mainly

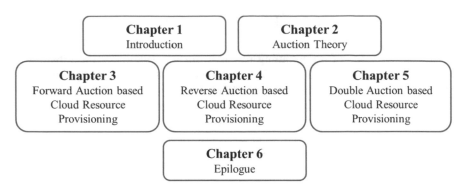

Fig. 1.4 Book organization

categorized in three classes on the basis of the role of customer and the provider: forward auction, reverse auction and double auction. Chapter 3 deals with the forward auction in which the resources are allocated to those users who value them the most in a competitive scenario. Chapter 4 deliberates on reverse auction in which customer selects that provider who offers the required resources at lowest price. Chapter 5 is dedicated to double auction which is a matching problem between providers and customers. These three chapters not only discuss about the existing works available in literature but also formulate the resource allocation problem. This is a great deal for the readers as they will be able to understand exactly the feasibility of auction in Cloud.

Figure 1.4 depicts the organization of the book. This chapter and Chap. 2 are disjoint in nature. Readers can pick any one to start according to their interest. Same way Chaps. 3–5 are independent with each other and can be read in any sequence but all three requires a proper understanding of this chapter and Chap. 2 both.

Chapter 1 provides a brief introduction of Cloud computing to create a sufficient background for the reader. This chapter also provides motivation behind the book by explaining research challenges in resource provisioning problem in Cloud computing for which auction can be a suitable mechanism. Further, this chapter chalks out the organization of the book.

Chapter 2 is dedicated to auction in general. One will get sufficient knowledge of auction from this chapter which will help in reading and understanding of further chapters.

In Chap. 3, forward auction is discussed in detail. Benefits of forward auction for customer and provider have also been given. Available literature on forward auction has been discussed in this chapter. A combinatorial auction-based formulation is given for VM Provisioning and Pricing problem in the Cloud market. Open issues have been discussed at the end.

Chapter 4 provides a detailed description of reverse auction in Cloud computing and its benefits to Cloud customers and providers. Current works, related to procurement of resources in Cloud computing using reverse auction, are provided followed by the formulation of combinatorial reverse auction problem. At the end, challenges in reverse auction are listed to call upon researchers for providing solutions.

Chapter 5 is dedicated to double auction. In this chapter, benefits of double auction for Cloud customer and Cloud provider have been discussed. Existing related works, formulation of double auction problem, and challenges in double auction have also been deliberated.

Chapter 6 discusses about Amazon spot market to provide a view of real implementation of auction in Cloud. This chapter summarizes the work and briefly recalls everything that have been discussed in previous chapters. This chapter also suggests various literature and resources to probe further. It helps to develop a framework of learning obtained from this book.

Chapter 2
Auction Theory

Abstract Auctioning has a long history and is reported to have been used in Babylon as early as 500 B.C. The entire Roman Empire was sold off using auction in 193 A.D. [83]. With time, auction theory has evolved with more sophisticated and mature auction procedures. Auction is considered as an efficient and fair mechanism as it provides equal opportunity to both the seller and the buyer. The price of the resources is decided on the basis of the value of the resources for the bidders that makes higher revenue. In early auction days and even during its evolution, only antiques and art matters were sold using auction but now various commodities, e.g. fish, bond, spectrum, computing resources, are sold using auction because of its multifaceted benefits. After the introduction of mechanism design, auction has become a great success in economics for the resource allocation. Mechanism design and information and communication technologies (ICTs) are the two major responsible factors that made game theory and optimization an effective tool for auction design to achieve specific goals. In economics, the rich literature and practical implementation on auction are available. Because of involvement of pricing in resource allocation in Cloud computing, good possibilities can be explored for applying auction in Cloud computing. Academicians have proposed various types of auction models that can be applied in different scenarios in Cloud computing. Spot market has been become a milestone for both, academicians and professionals, to explore auction in greater depth. Amazon, a giant in the Cloud computing market, practically gave a push to implement dynamic pricing using auction. Plenty of works on auction theory, variants of auction as well as its applications for suitable scenario are available in the form of books, survey papers, etc. The aim of this chapter is to provide a detailed description of most important findings of the auction so that academicians and researchers can work their way through these findings in Cloud computing.

© The Author(s) 2018
G. Baranwal et al., *Auction Based Resource Provisioning in Cloud Computing*,
SpringerBriefs in Computer Science, https://doi.org/10.1007/978-981-10-8737-0_2

2.1   Introduction

Auction is also known as market-clearing mechanism that equates demand and supply [111]. Process of pricing of resources in auction is very clear; i.e., each participant is well aware of the rules of pricing formation. G. Anandalingam et al. define auction as *"An auction is a mechanism of information submission, together with rules for assigning items and payments to participants based on this submitted information"* [6].

R. L. Zhan explains auction in very simple words that are easy to understand to even naïve readers *"An auction is a game with partial information where a player's valuation of an object is hidden from other players. It serves as a popular method in resources (goods) allocation to specify a set of rules to determine the winner(s) and the related payments. A typical setting of the auction is that a seller attempts to sell one or more items to a set of bidders. The involved players (seller and bidders) do not have complete information about the value of the items on sale in the sense that they do not know others' values but know their own values, which may or may not be affected by others. All players are assumed to be selfish and pay-off-maximizing. The auction theory studies the behaviour of the players in this non-cooperative environment"* [211].

According to [80], there are two main reasons for the wide acceptance of auction among the researchers. First, the rules of auction are simple and it provides useful and elegant results. Second, auction is very useful and widely practiced ancient market mechanism. These reasons are the driving force for the possible implementation of auction in Cloud computing. Auction has been used effectively and efficiently for spectrum allocation in mobile communication, to trade-off electricity using spot marketing, for procurement of resources in government organizations, and many more. Currently, spot instances by Amazon apply auction in Cloud computing. Though spot instances are implementation of forward auction, academicians and professionals are working hard to implement other variants of auction such as online auction, reverse auction, double auction in Cloud computing by proposing various mathematical models [192]. Hurwicz, Maskin and Myerson received Nobel Prize in economics in 2007 for their contribution in mechanism design [181]. Mechanism design helps in drafting economic policy to fetch the desired objectives. Mechanism design also called as "Reverse Game Theory" then acted as a booster for the academicians and professionals as it makes possible to design auction with desired objectives.

2.2   Entities in Auction

Three important entities, in any auction, are: seller, buyer and auctioneer.

Seller

Seller owns the commodities, offers them to the customer (buyer) and in return makes profit in terms of money. In Cloud computing, Cloud providers are basically the sellers and computing resources such as various types of VMs are the commodities. The terms Cloud provider, Cloud service provider and provider are used as the synonyms for the "seller" in this work.

Buyer

Buyer purchases the commodities from the sellers. In Cloud computing, Cloud customer is the buyer who wants computing resources to execute its job and pays price in return. The terms Cloud customer, Cloud user, customer and user are used as the synonyms for the "buyer" in this work.

Auctioneer

Auctioneer is an intermediate agent who performs the auction and is considered as the most important entity. It basically acts as the market maker. A study in economics suggests that auctioneer can improve the liquidity and the economic efficiency of the market [28]. Since auctioneer has the repository of the historical transactions, it can help sellers to identify the new trends during provisioning and resource allocation [42].

2.3   Steps In Auction

Generally, auctions are performed by two sub-processes: winner determination and payment mechanism. According to [90, 92], there are six steps in auction. These steps are described below.

Step 1: Bid Collection and Validation

First step, in the auction process, is to collect the bids from various bidders by the auctioneer. Rules and constraints need to be specified clearly for the eligibility of the bid or bidder; e.g., a bid may be firm or may be changeable. Other constraints may be bid expiry, resource availability, bidder's budget, time period for which resources are needed, etc. In validation phase, auctioneer cancels those bids which do not meet the required specifications for the bid.

Step 2: Auction Close

Auctioneer may close accepting the bids depending upon certain conditions. These conditions may be sufficient number of bids received, time limit specified for bidding, availability of resources, etc. After closing the auction, any change in a bid or accepting new bids would not be possible.

Step 3: Valuation and Bid ranking

After closing the auction, auctioneer computes the value of each bid. On the basis of the bid value, bidders are sorted, i.e. ranked. The value of bid can be different in different scenarios. For example, in case of uni-attribute forward auction, price of resource in the bid is the value of that bid. Bidders are sorted in decreasing order of value of bids, i.e. price. In case of multi-attribute auction, non-price attributes need to be incorporated while defining the bid value using some rules. As per need, these rules may be published publically or kept anonymous.

Step 4: Resource Ranking

Intrinsic value of resource may be equal or different for the available resources in the auction. For example, in cinema hall, intrinsic value of seats changes with distance between screen and seats. Resources available, for current round of auction, are ranked according to their intrinsic value. In other words, the ranking of the resources reflects their intrinsic value.

Step 5: Winner Determination

In this step, some bidders are selected as winners for the resource allocation based on the predefined rules. Computational complexity of the winner determination process increases with the increase in the number of bidders, i.e. number of participants in the market.

Step 6: Payment Mechanism

After winner determination, customer pays on the basis of defined pricing mechanism to the provider in order to avail the services. A proper implementation of pricing scheme can make auction truthful, i.e. incentive compatible.

Though payment is considered as the last step, some of the works consider one more step, i.e. price settlement [18, 20, 142]. In this, if at the end it is observed that the seller or the buyer cheats, some penalty is imposed. Buyer or seller has to pay according to some new calculated price by incorporating some penalty on the participants.

2.4 Categorization of Auction

A steady growth has been observed in the field of resource allocation using auction. Internet is one of the strongest factors that have contributed in this growth. Internet not only made communication cost close to zero for supply and demand of the resources but also eliminated geographical barriers in the market. With the time, auction has evolved and more sophisticated auction mechanisms were designed to increase and promote the efficient allocation of the resources. Various other market scenarios apply auction for the allocation of the resources. Even various governments are using the auction for the allocation of the resources in highly uncertain environment. Few common resources, for which auction has been successfully implemented, are bonds, electricity, fish, airport slot, real estate, radio spectrum, etc. In this era, where privacy has become a commodity, practitioners are claiming that auction can be helpful in selling the private information [64].

There are various possibilities for the categorization of the auction on the basis of several distinct criteria (market scenario) [111, 143]. Few identified categorizations, available in the literature, are listed as follows.

2.4.1 On the Basis of Role of Participants

Forward Auction

In this, buyers compete with each other to get the resources. In other words, buyers are the bidders. Auctioneer processes auction on behalf of the seller. Seller itself may play the role of the auctioneer. In forward auction, there are single seller and multiple competitive buyers.

Reverse Auction

Unlike forward auction, in reverse auction multiple sellers compete with each other to offer the resources to a buyer. Thus, sellers are the bidders. This auction is usually applied for the resource procurement. In this, buyer itself may be the auctioneer or can submit its requirements to the auctioneer for the processing of the auction. Therefore, there is a single customer and multiple rational and self-interested sellers.

Double Auction

In double auction, both sellers and buyers bid. Basically, it is a matching problem. The literature says that auctioneer is an independent entity in the double auction.

2.4.2 On the Basis of Bidding Side

One-Side Auction

When only sellers or only buyers bid, i.e. compete among themselves to do the business. Forward and reverse auctions are single-sided auctions.

Double-Sided Auction

Bidding is done from both the sides, i.e. from the seller side and the buyer side. This auction is also called as double auction.

2.4.3 On the Basis of Resources

Single-Unit Single-Item

When single type of resource and single quantity of that resource is available for bidding.

Multi-unit Single-Item

When quantity of resource can be more than one but of a single type of resource.

Single-Unit Multi-item

When multiple types of resources are available but quantity of all types of resources is only one.

Multi-unit Multi-item

When more than one type of resources are available and multiple quantities of these resources can be auctioned.

2.4.4 On the Basis of Bid Composition

Uni-attribute

This is also called as single-dimensional auction. In this, winner is decided on the basis of the price only. Bid is composed of price only.

Multi-attribute

In multi-attribute auction, also called as multidimensional auction, non-price attributes also matter besides the price. Bid is composed of price and various non-price attributes such as quality, response time. Winner determination decision depends on multi-attributes.

2.4.5 On the Basis of Pricing Mechanism

First Pricing

In the first-price forward auction, buyer with highest bid wins the auction and has to pay the exact amount offered in its bid. While in the first-price reverse auction, seller with lowest bid wins the auction and gets the exact amount mentioned in its bid by the buyer.

Second Pricing

Second pricing is used to give some incentive to the bidders to reveal their true value in their bids. Winner gets second lowest price in the reverse auction, while winner has to pay second highest price in the forward auction. This is also known as Vickrey auction [186].

Kth Pricing

In Kth pricing, a buyer/supplier winner pays/gets paid the Kth highest price. In second pricing, the value of K is 2. This pricing scheme is used in multi-unit auction.

VCG Auction

In VCG auction, resources are allocated in a socially optimal manner (welfare maximizing) by giving incentives to the bidder to bid truthfully. VCG auctions are efficient and truthful and are special applications of VCG mechanisms [45, 67, 128, 186].

One can argue that first pricing is better than second pricing because in first-pricing forward auction, seller would get more revenue as compared to second pricing. Also, in first-pricing reverse auction, buyer will get the resources at lesser price as compared to second pricing. But [111] has shown that bidders bid less than true valuation in the first-price auction, while bidders bid their true valuation in the second-price auction.

2.4.6 On the Basis of Information Feedback

Dynamic Auction

Auction allows multiple bidding from the bidders. To achieve transparency, some private information such as privacy of the bidders is disclosed. This is also known as open-cry or open-bid auction. Bidders openly call out their bids, i.e. reveal their preferences in the market. There are two types of bidding as follows [118].

- *Bids at discrete rounds*: It is also known as iterative auction in which bidders can modify their bids after knowing others' bid during iteration.
- *Continuous Auction*: Bids are provided by the bidders on continuous basis.

Sealed Bid

To preserve privacy, bidders submit their bids secretly to the auctioneer; i.e., none of the bidders have idea about others' bids.

Price discovery is the main advantage of dynamic auction. Because bidders will be able to know the valuation of their opponents, it reduces the uncertainty which in turn reduces the effect of winner's curse [31]. The disadvantage is that bidders with low bid will avoid the auction and monopoly of the strong bidders may increase. Also, the auction process may be long resulting in costly auction. While sealed-bid auction is not only quick but also reduces the collusion among the bidders. However, the disadvantage with seal bid auction is that the revenue of the seller may decrease in case of forward auction. It is because bidders may try to make low bids to reduce the winner's curse problem. Same may happen in reverse and double auction as well.

2.4.7   On the Basis of Bid Structure

Single-unit single-item auction follows a simple structure of auction because of single unit of resources, and absence of complex business constraints such as resources may be complimentary, etc. Incorporation of these constraints in a bid improves the relationship between the seller and the buyer. Sometimes, these constraints are more important than price [72].

Volume Discount Auction

For multi-unit auction, rules may be different. Multi-unit auction needs to specify quantity and price both. A price can be slashed if the volume of the resource increases. Such type of auction is called volume discount auction; i.e., a volume discount is offered.

Auction with Single-Minded Bidder

It is possible that a bidder specifies all-or-nothing constraints. Such type of bidder is called single-minded bidder.

Combinatorial Auction

In this type of auction, a collection of resources is available in the form of a bundle. Resources in the bundle are dependent and complimentary.

2.4.8 Ascending and Descending Auctions

Ascending Auction

In ascending auction, auctioneer entertains the bids and bidders keep on increasing their bid value above the highest available bid. Auction stops if no bidder is willing to increase the bid and the current highest bidder becomes the winner. This is also called English auction.

Descending Auction

In this, unlike English auction, auctioneer sets a high bid price and lowers it until some participant accepts the price. The characteristics of both, the descending and the ascending auctions, suggest that both of these need to be an open auction.

In both these auctions, prices can be changed steadily (clock auction) by the bidders or by the auctioneer. Since both are open-cry auction, they inherit the advantage and the disadvantage of an open-cry auction, i.e. reduced winner's curse problem and long auction period, respectively. Second pricing is also possible in both; it would encourage bidders to reveal their true value.

2.4.9 Reserve Price Auction and Entry Fee Auction

Reserve Price Auction

In reserve price auction, the seller declares a reserve price; i.e., selling the resources below this price would not be possible by the seller [118]. Deciding an optimal reserve price is a non-trivial task [118]. Studies, such as [56], provide an analysis of determining optimal reserve price in different scenarios of auction. In forward auction, seller can make this reserve price public or private. In case of private reserve price, seller may inform bidders about the implementation of reserve price but not the amount. Sometimes, bidders may not know the implementation of reserve price at all. However, in case of public reserve price, bidders know about this reserve price; i.e., reserve price is minimum bid or reserve price is starting bid.

Benefits of private reserve price are that losing bidder of the previous round may participate in the current round and expect to win because they do not know the value of the reserve price at all [118]. Another possibility is that bidders may think that submitting low bids would not keep them in the competition and therefore would discourage them. Another approach to sell resources at handsome price is shill bids [39]. It introduces artificial bidders in auction. In general, auction prohibits this.

Entry Fee Auction

In entry fee auction, bidders have to pay an entry fee to participate in the auction. Penny auction is an example of such type of auction [126].

In both auctions, pricing is more like monopolist pricing. These auctions are not efficient, but revenue of a seller can be improved in these auctions.

Though in this chapter various categories of auction that have been deliberated, applying auction in Cloud computing is in nascent stage and most of the existing works can be categorized in forward auction, reverse auction and double auction on the basis of the role of participants. Next three chapters are based on these types of auction only. However, description of other categories of auction will motivate the Cloud researchers to find suitable scenario in Cloud in which these can be applied.

2.5   Auction and Mechanism Design

In this section, some fundamental concepts of mechanism design are discussed along with their desirable properties, design components, impossibility results, environments, etc. Special emphasis is given to auction, an application of mechanism design.

In auction, sellers and buyers, both the participants, are autonomous, rational and intelligent. Here, autonomous means they are not bound to act according to the instruction of the central authority (in this case auctioneer), rational means both are self-interested, i.e. they are participating in the auction to optimize their objectives, and intelligent means they are capable to decide their action on the basis of their own knowledge and expected behaviour of auctioneer and other participants. For example, in forward auction, provider acts as an auctioneer while customers are bidders. In forward auction, objective of customers is to minimize the payment for the required resources. Often customers are reluctant to reveal their true value for the required resources. In this case, provider may not get the best price of the resources. Same is true for reverse auction and double auction. In reverse auction, providers will try to obfuscate information to maximize their revenue, while in double auction both buyers and sellers may try to hide their true information in order to increase their utility.

In the above situation, where participants avoid revealing their true information and are autonomous, rational and intelligent, mechanism design can be applied. Mechanism design helps central authority to design rules using which participants interact with each other in their own interest in achieving globally desirable outcome. Mechanism design also helps central authority to reveal actual information of the participants needed for the globally desirable objectives.

2.5.1   Basics of Mechanism Design

Mechanism design works in the environment of non-cooperative games where players act strategically and may hide some information, revelation of which helps to achieve the desired outcome. Mechanism design helps in the formation of such institution or protocols that seek elicitation of private information possessed by participants to achieve the desired objectives assuming that participants will interact strategically. The popularity and importance of mechanism design, in applied economics and market-driven applications, can be understood by the fact that Roger Myerson, Leonid Hurwicz and Eric Maskin were awarded Nobel Prize in economics in 2007 for their contribution in the field of mechanism design.

Mechanism design, mainly used in micro-economics, has a major impact on policy making and a breakthrough in the study of institutions and markets. Most of its fundamentals are based on game theory. Recently, mechanism design is extensively used for many computer science problems like distributed resource allocation (spectrum, radio, virtualized resources, etc.), online advertising, electronic market design, sponsored search auction design. The detailed literature on mechanism design in economics can be found in [105] (Chap. 23), [136] (Chap. 10). A good introduction of mechanism design with its application in computer science is given in [134, 133] (Chap. 9) [128].

Narahari et al. in their book "Game Theory and Mechanism Design" clearly defined the relation between the game theory [136] and mechanism design [134] as follows.

> While game theory focuses on analysis of games, mechanism design is concerned with design of games to obtain desirable outcomes. Mechanism design can be viewed as the reverse engineering of games or equivalently as the art of designing the rules of a game to achieve a specific desired outcome.

Basic Model of Mechanism Design: Framework and Environment

Let there are n rational and intelligent agents in a strategic environment and $N = \{1, 2, \ldots, n\}$, where N is the set of agents. These agents interact with each other strategically to achieve a global objective or social goal. Let X be the set of possible outcomes or alternatives from which agents have to make a collective choice. Each agent has some preferences over the outcomes in the set X which is a private information and known to the agent himself. This private information is denoted by θ_i and called as *type* of agent i. Let $\ominus = \ominus_1 \times \ominus_2 \times \cdots \times \ominus_n$ is the set of type profiles of all agents where $\ominus_i$ is the type space of agent i and denotes the set of all private values of agent i. The planner or mechanism designer has information about $\ominus_i$ but does not know θ_i. An agent evaluates his preferences over different outcomes using a utility function $u_i : X \times \ominus_i \to \mathbb{R}$. Here, $u_i(x, \theta_i)$ denotes the utility/payoff gain by agent i when outcome is $x \in X$ and his type is θ_i. All mechanisms can be categorized into two types: "*mechanisms with transfers*" and "*mechanisms without transfers*". Voting mechanisms and matching mechanisms are examples of "mechanisms without transfers". Auction is a special example of "*mechanisms with transfers*".

Social Choice Function (SCF)

A social choice function (SCF) is a map $f : \ominus \to X$ that assigns an outcome to every type profile of agents. In this regard, the outcome corresponding to a type profile is called collective choice or social choice. A social choice function must be designed in such a way that it captures the objectives of a mechanism designer.

In case of "*mechanisms with transfers*", e.g. in auction, a SCF can be interpreted as $(f, p_1, \ldots, p_n)$ where $f : \ominus \rightarrow X$ is the allocation function and $p_i : \ominus \rightarrow \mathbb{R}$ is the payment decision rule. The utility of an agent i can be calculated as follows: $U_i\left(\hat{\theta}, \theta_i; f\right) = u_i\left(f\left(\hat{\theta}\right), \theta_i\right)$ where $\hat{\theta}$ is the reported type of agent i to the SCF.

A mechanism design is a process of designing interaction among the agents that achieves a system-wide objective by eliciting the private types of agents. A mechanism can be used for the realization of the outcomes of a social choice function. This can be done in two different ways: direct mechanisms and indirect mechanisms. A direct mechanism corresponds to a SCF f is a tuple $(\ominus_1, \ominus_2, \ldots, \ominus_n, f(.))$; i.e. mechanism designer directly seeks the private types from each agent by asking them to reveal their true types. An indirect mechanism can be represented as a tuple $(S_1, S_2, \ldots, S_n, g(.))$. Here, S_i denotes the set of all possible actions agent i can perform and $g : S_1 \times S_2 \times \cdots \times S_n \rightarrow X$ is a mapping function similar to SCF f that maps each action profiles to an outcome. In case of direct mechanism, $S_i = \ominus_i \ \forall i \in N$ and $g = f$. Main difference between these two mechanisms is the way in which individual types are communicated to the designer. In a direct mechanism, a designer tries to extract private types truthfully from agents by implementing SCF f in dominant strategies. In indirect mechanisms, designer gives incentives to the agents in order to extract truthful information from them.

2.5.2   *Mechanism Design for Auction*

Auction is one of the many applications of the mechanism design that has been used extensively in different domains for allocation. The mechanism design problem is formulated to find the allocation of some objects/resources among the bidders given that value of the resource is known to the bidder only. Here, global objectives or social goals may be maximizing the revenue of seller or maximizing the total social welfare (resources are allocated to those bidders who value them the most) in the auction-based market. Mechanism design problem in auction is mainly analysing the behaviour of particular mechanisms (e.g. first-price auction, second-price auction), and focus is given to designing auctions from the view of welfare maximization or revenue maximization with some other desirable properties. The following is a single-object procurement auction (reverse auction) which is discussed from mechanism design point of view.

Example: Single-Object Procurement

Consider to procure a Cloud resource (e.g. VM) from multiple sellers, i.e. Cloud service providers in the competitive market. This involves the case of monetary transfers and comes into the class of "*mechanism design with transfers*". In this, an outcome consists of two components: allocation decision $\mathcal{A}$ and payment decision $\mathcal{P}$. An outcome, thus, consists of two vectors $(\mathcal{A}, \mathcal{P})$, where $\mathcal{A} = \{a_1, a_2, \ldots, a_n\}$, $a_i \in \{0, 1\} \ \forall i \in N$ and $\sum_{i \in N} a_i \leq 1$ and Payment vector $\mathcal{P} = (p_1, p_2, \ldots, p_N)$ denotes the payment each seller receives. Therefore, in this scenario, X is the set of all pairs of $(\mathcal{A}, \mathcal{P})$, θ_i is the ask price/cost of seller i for the object, and quasi-linear utility function in this scenario is $u_i((\mathcal{A}, \mathcal{P}), \theta_i) = p_i - a_i \theta_i$.

The above auction environment is reverse auction with single resource for procurement. Other types of auction, with different assumptions, can be modelled in a similar way using the mechanism design framework.

2.6   Properties of Auction Mechanism

In the literature, various properties of auction have been mentioned that help auction designer to evaluate the designed auction, which have been discussed as follows.

Incentive Compatibility

An auction mechanism is said to be incentive compatible (also known as truthfulness or strategy proof), when bidders get maximum utility by truthful bidding, i.e. revealing their true information, though they act strategically. Designing of payment mechanism can help auction designer to achieve this. [93] suggested that an auction should have following four properties to ensure truthfulness in auction: exactness, monotonicity, critical payment and participation. A detailed discussion about these four properties can be found in [93]. There are two forms of incentive compatibility.

- *Dominant strategy incentive compatibility*: When bidders get maximum utility by revealing their true information irrespective of the bids from other bidders.
- *Bayesian-Nash incentive compatibility*: It is a weaker form compared to the former. In this, a bidder reveals its private information when other bidders also reveal their private information.

In the mechanism design literature, Vickrey, Clarke and Groves developed market-based mechanisms widely known as VCG mechanisms [45, 67, 186]. These mechanisms are both allocative efficient and truthful in quasi-linear environment. Groves' mechanisms are the most generalized ones in quasi-linear environment, whereas Clarke's mechanism is a special case of Groves' mechanisms. When Clarke's mechanisms are used in combinatorial auction, they are called generalized Vickrey auction (GVA) mechanisms [185]. Vickrey auction is similar to second-price sealed-bid auction of a single individual good [186].

Individual Rationality

An auction is individual rational if participants in auction get nonnegative utility whether they win or lose. The objective behind this property is to motivate the participants to take part in the auction.

Optimality

In forward auction, goal of the seller is to maximize its revenue which could be possible when seller gets highest bid as payment. If this is the case, then this auction holds optimal property. Same applies for the reverse auction; i.e., reverse auction is optimal when customer pays lowest bid. But to ensure truthfulness in the auction, auctioneer needs to give some incentive to bidders; i.e., optimality may be affected in this case.

Efficiency

Efficiency is explained, in the literature on auction, in various ways. One notion of measurement of efficiency is in terms of social welfare. In this, auction is called efficient when business is done with the best participants. For example, a reverse auction is called efficient when resources are purchased by the seller who is offering the resources at lowest price. Another notion of efficiency is allocative efficiency, when auction maximizes the utility of the whole system, i.e. aggregated utility of all participants rather than an individual.

Budget-Balance

An auction holds this property if sum of the payments made by the customers is greater than or equal to the sum of the payments received by the providers. In other words, difference of former and later quantity is greater than or equal to zero. Auction is said to be exactly budget-balanced when this difference is zero, whereas when difference is positive, auction is called weakly budget-balanced. The objective behind this property is to motivate the auctioneer to process the auction. It can be observed that budget-balance property holds individual rationality for the auctioneer while auctioneer is not a participant. Budget-balance is an important property for double auction because in double auction, auctioneer is an independent entity. For single-sided auction, budget-balance does not play a significant role if seller is auctioneer in forward auction and buyer is auctioneer in reverse auction.

Computational Complexity

It may also be called time complexity. It represents the amount of time taken by the auction. Time complexity increases as the size of the problem increases. Few applications may demand fast algorithm for auction. Therefore, auction mechanism must be computationally tractable. In the literature, it is found that combinatorial auction is NP-hard problem [2]. Algorithms need to be designed in such a way that they should be computationally tractable.

Fairness

Universally accepted definition of fairness is not available. This is subjective and researchers may have different opinions about this. [169] have given a survey on fairness in wireless networks and quoted various definitions of fairness such as "*an allocation where no person in the economy prefers anyone else's consumption bundle over his own*" [117], "*A fair allocation is free of envy*" [51] and "*Equal treatment to every individuals and reserving preferred treatment for those individuals who are in some sense more deserving*" [164]. Various definitions of fairness make it fuzzy, but making a just distribution of resources to make just society seems acceptable as a sense of fairness for everyone. In this section, fairness in social welfare is considered as auction property Fairness can be understood as welfare of participants involved in the auction. Generally, it can be defined in two ways: utilitarian and egalitarian [55]. In utilitarian view of social welfare, mechanism tries to maximize the individual's welfare. It does not care for the difference generated among individuals. While in egalitarian view of social welfare, sum of individuals' welfare is maximized. It also reduces the difference among the participants or the individuals. It can be observed that egalitarian social welfare is more justifiable to provide fairness.

Any auction designer would like to have all the properties in its designed auction. But researchers proved that it is not just possible [125]. As discussed, generally optimality cannot be achieved without sacrificing truthfulness in the system. Individual rationality can be expected in each auction because this is a motivation factor for the participants. Any auctioneer will not perform auction voluntarily, that is why budget-balance is also expected in each auction. Combinatorial auctions are NP-hard problems. For small instances of the problem, execution time is not an issue but for large instances sub-optimal solution should be acceptable in order to obtain the result in limited time. Same as to make system fair, again optimal solution may not be acceptable. But in long term, fairness is very much beneficial as it maintains a healthy completion in the system. Any auction designer must understand what properties are necessary for the system towards which they are working.

VCG mechanisms are the most important class of mechanisms which are individual rational, truthful and socially optimal (Social Welfare maximizing). In VCG auction, bidding with true information is a dominant strategy for each participant. These mechanisms are the most efficient [135] among all truthful mechanisms proposed in the literature.

2.7 Summary

Allocation of resources using auction is not new, but introduction of mechanism design gives a new perspective to this method. In Cloud computing, this is an active area of research. This chapter provides a basic understanding of auction for Cloud computing researchers. Few well-accepted definitions are given followed by the description of the entities involved in the auction. This will help the readers to map the entities of Cloud to the entities in the auction and their roles. The literature provides various categorizations of auction which have also been briefed. A rich literature of mechanism design and its applications are available; therefore, only few mechanism design and auction as its application have been briefed for the completeness of this chapter. This chapter also describes various auction properties. Going through this, researchers will be able to fully understand what they can expect from their designed auction. Overall, this chapter along with Chap. 1 provides sufficient background to understand the forthcoming chapters.

Chapter 3
Forward Auction-Based Cloud Resource Provisioning

Abstract Forward auction, also known as "sell-side auction", has multiple buyers and single seller in the auction market. The buyers compete by bidding their valuations for the required quantity of resources. In Cloud computing, Amazon sells its unutilized capacity using forward auction. In this chapter, a description of combinatorial forward auction with their relevance and applicability in Cloud is discussed in detail. A combinatorial auction-based formulation is given for the VM provisioning and pricing problem in Cloud market. Some possible allocation algorithms and pricing schemes are discussed for the formulated problem. A detailed survey of existing combinatorial auction mechanisms in Cloud computing is given. Finally, research challenges and issues are discussed to explore future possibilities.

3.1 Introduction

At present, there are quite a few service providers who offer their services using more than one pricing scheme. Recently, Amazon has started offering their unutilized capacity using a forward auction-based pricing mechanism called spot pricing [12]. Amazon spot users bid the quantity and the valuation of the spot VMs they require. Amazon derives a spot price after analysing all the submitted bids. The users who bid more than the spot price get the resources successfully, while losing bidders may bid again in the next round of the auction if they desire so.

All users in the Cloud market compete with each other to access the limited amount of resources (i.e. unutilized resources of the providers) at minimum cost and desired QoS. Cloud providers, in this case, try to maximize their revenue by selling more VMs provisioned from their servers at optimal price with expected QoS. This type of market environment can be modelled using forward auction, where bidding happens from the users' side. These types of auction can be used to design optimal allocation and pricing strategy which are able to fulfil the objectives of both the user and the provider.

Resource allocation models, based on forward auction, have been proposed in Cloud computing domain as available in the literature. In these models, various

© The Author(s) 2018

G. Baranwal et al., *Auction Based Resource Provisioning in Cloud Computing*,
SpringerBriefs in Computer Science, https://doi.org/10.1007/978-981-10-8737-0_3

allocation and pricing mechanisms have been designed using number of methods such as optimization techniques, heuristics, approximations. Moreover, both resource allocation and pricing should be seen as a unified mechanism. Forward auction, from a mechanism design point of view, has mainly two phases: *allocation phase* and *pricing phase*. Cloud users submit bids to the auctioneer/broker/provider. After analysing all the bids, provider finds the winning users in *allocation phase*. The resources are allocated to the winning users, and payment is determined in the *pricing phase*. A key point here is that outcome of the *pricing phase* depends on the *allocation phase*. As discussed earlier, an auction mechanism should possess certain properties such as economic and computational efficiency, truthfulness, individual rationality. Therefore, allocation and payment schemes both need to be designed in such a way that the whole mechanism satisfies the above-said properties. The payment scheme depends upon the allocation method used in the mechanism.

Since Amazon started offering resources (called spot instances), various forward auction-based mechanisms (most of them considered the combinatorial bidding) have been proposed in the literature. Although these mechanisms claim good allocation efficiency and satisfying various economic properties, most of them failed for actual implementation. It is because the assumptions considered in these works do not fit into the real Cloud market scenario. This motivates the researchers to design combinatorial auction-based allocation and pricing mechanisms for Cloud computing. This also encourages industry professionals to give alternatives to Amazon SIs by providing Cloud services based on auction model.

In this chapter, we investigate several truthful combinatorial auction-based resource allocation and pricing mechanisms in Cloud computing. The aim of this chapter is to provide background, up-to-date references on combinatorial auction-based models in Cloud computing, and open problems that appears to provide good opportunities for computer scientists and economists to explore the fascinating field of Cloud market design using combinatorial forward auction. Designing efficient (allocative as well as computational) and truthful combinatorial auction mechanisms is the main theme of this chapter.

The rest of the chapter is as follows. A detailed study on basic combinatorial auction mechanisms with their properties and specially truthfulness in combinatorial auction is presented in Sect. 3.2. In Sect. 3.3, a combinatorial auction-based framework for the Cloud market is presented along with the discussion on the applicability of these auctions in Cloud computing environment. A formulation of combinatorial auction-based VM provisioning and pricing problem is given in Sect. 3.4 along with possible allocation algorithms and pricing schemes. Various issues and challenges for the combinatorial forward auction-based Cloud computing market are presented in Sect. 3.5. Section 3.6 summarizes the chapter.

3.2 Combinatorial Forward Auction

Forward auctions, also known as "sell-side auction", can be used for allocating resources/goods in a competitive market with multiple buyers and single seller. In combinatorial forward auction, Cloud users have preferences over a combination of resources; i.e., they have a single valuation for a bundle of resources. Generally, in combinatorial forward auction, a Cloud user is single-minded; i.e., user will pay if it gets the complete bundle; otherwise, it pays nothing. Combinatorial auction is applicable for those goods or objects which have two properties: complementarity and substitutability. The two items are called complementary to each other if the value of one item increases when it is consumed along with the other. An item which can be used in place of another is called substitute item of the other item. If these two properties do not exist, then combinatorial auction is equivalent to multiple auction as a set of independent single-/multi-unit auctions. Suppose there are two sets of resources s_1 and s_2 and $v_i(s_k)$ is the valuation of ith user for kth set of resources. Complementarity property satisfies the following $v_i(s_1 \cup s_2) > v_i(s_1) + v_i(s_2)$ and Substitutability ensures that $v_i(s_1 \cup s_2) < v_i(s_1) + v_i(s_2)$ [50].

Combinatorial auctions are being studied exclusively since long due to its wider applicability in various domains. A multi-item combinatorial auction with integer linear programming (ILP) technique was first formulated in [151] for airport time slot allocation. In this work, authors proved the efficiency of combinatorial auction over non-combinatorial auction by experimentation on various test subjects. Ball et al. [15] and Gruyer and Lenoir [69] further studied the combinatorial auction for airport time slot allocation by giving emphasis on economic benefits of using combinatorial auction as compared to other allocation methods. Combinatorial auctions were also used in some other government-controlled allocation mechanisms such as auctions in treasury, electricity, equity trading, transportation exchange, pollution rights. Spectrum allocation is one of the important domains, in government-controlled allocations, where combinatorial auction has been extensively used [101]. While solving the winner determination problem (WDP) in combinatorial auction, some works such as [154] restricted the set of items on which bids can be placed. These types of auctions are called restricted subset combinatorial auction for which WDP problem can be solved in polynomial time.

3.2.1 Design Goals and Auction Properties

A forward auction-based market mechanism aims certain objectives such as economic efficiency, optimality, truthfulness, computational efficiency. depending upon the application domain. Revenue maximization is the aim of the provider whereas efficiency (social welfare maximization) is what provider expects [99, 125]. For revenue/profit maximization, allocation function and payment schemes both are designed in such a way that the net revenue over a time horizon (e.g. 10 rounds of auction) is maximized. Myerson in 1981 designed an optimal auction mechanism for selling a single individual item which generates maximum revenue compared to all other contemporary mechanisms in the literature [124].

For efficiency, in order to maximize total social welfare, mechanism designer assigns the resources to the most eligible bidder (i.e. bidder with highest valuation) so that the sum of valuations of winning bidders is maximized. Vickrey auction is an example of such efficient mechanisms [186]. An efficient mechanism always results in the revenue maximization of the provider, but the reverse may not be true; i.e., a revenue maximization mechanism is not always efficient [124]. Computational efficiency is also an important requirement in the combinatorial auction. Truthfulness is another important requirement, while designing a forward auction-based mechanism, and is discussed in below section.

3.2.2   Truthfulness in Combinatorial Forward Auction

Truthfulness in combinatorial auction mechanism was addressed in [93] by designing approximately efficient allocation functions (greedy-based) and truthful second-pricing-based payments for users. The authors could present that standard mechanisms for combinatorial auction like generalized Vickrey auction (GVA), Vickrey–Clarke–Groves (VCG) mechanisms are not implementable as these mechanisms are computationally intractable. To obtain an optimal solution in polynomial time, for the winner determination problem in combinatorial auction, is computationally intractable. Therefore, to derive truthful auction mechanisms, both the allocation function and payment functions should be modified to ensure the truthfulness property. In [93], authors used the greedy method to allocate the items to the bidders. They assumed that bidders are single-minded. Bidders are sorted using their bidding density derived as bidding price divided by the bundle size. The greedy-based approach approximates the solution with a factor of $\sqrt{M}$ where M is the total number of items/goods available to a seller/provider. Authors in [93] further depicted that GVA payments cannot be used with the greedy allocation schemes. They detailed four properties to be satisfied for truthfulness for single-minded bidders. These properties are as follows.

Exactness

This property ensures that either a bidder gets its full requested bundle or nothing; i.e., if the bidder wins, it gets its bundle whose size is equal to or greater than the requested size, whereas if it loses, it gets nothing, i.e. zero.

Monotonicity

This property is related to the allocation function. The property ensures that a bidder gets more chance to win than some other bidder if its bidding price is more and bundle size is less; i.e., bid density (ratio of *price* and *bundle size*) of the bidder is more than the other bidders. For example, if ith bidder's bid is $\langle s_i, b_i \rangle$ where s_i is the bundle size and b_i is the bid price for that bundle, then the bidder will continue to win if it bids $\langle s_i', b_i' \rangle$ where $s_i' \subseteq s_i$ and $b_i' \geq b_i$. Meaning thereby that if a bidder is winning then even on changing the bids with higher price or fewer items, bidder will continue to win. Similarly, if a losing bidder bids lower prices or bids for more items, then in that case also, the bidder will be a loser.

Critical Payment

This property means that bidder's payment in auction mechanism does not depend upon its own bid value, but on other bidders' bid values as well. If a mechanism satisfies exactness and monotonicity, then for each bidder, there exists a critical value for which a bidder is a loser if the bidder bids less than that critical value or wins if the bidder bids more than that critical value.

Participation

This property is related to the payment schemes. The property implies that a bidder does not incur loss by participating in the auction; i.e., utility of each truthful bidder is nonnegative. If a bidder loses in the auction, the bidder pays zero; otherwise, it pays according to the payment schemes, but not more than its valuation.

If the above four properties are present in a mechanism, the mechanism is incentive compatible, i.e. truthful.

3.3 Basic Framework of Combinatorial Forward Auction-Based Cloud Market

Let us consider a Cloud provider which provides a variety of VM instance types suitable for different services/applications. These VMs comprise of varying combination of CPU, memory, storage, networking capacity, etc., which gives Cloud user the flexibility to choose an appropriate instance type for their applications. A Cloud user can be a business organization, institution or an ordinary customer that requires resources (VMs) to run its heterogeneous applications or to host its services. These types of users compete with each other to obtain the limited Cloud resources at minimum cost with desired QoS. Depending upon the tasks or applications' requirement, a user can generate a request for set of VMs which comprises of various resources provided by the Cloud provider. A user requests bundles of heterogeneous VM instances; i.e., user may have the requirements of communication-intensive as well as computation-intensive VMs. Depending upon the generated bundle, a bid value can be generated which depends upon the budget of the Cloud user. That bid value is private information to the Cloud user.

We assume that there are no externalities in the auction system; i.e., a Cloud user is concerned only about its requested resources. The allocation of resources to the other bidders does not affect the strategies of an individual bidder. It is also assumed that Cloud users are single-minded; i.e., for a requested set of VMs, a user gets positive utility only when it gets its complete bundle and otherwise gets zero utility. In

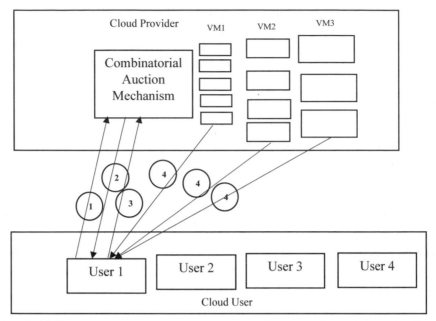

Step 1: All Cloud users submit the bids to Cloud provider. **Step 2:** Provider calculates allocation and payment and informs it to the user. **Step 3:** Winning User pay to the Cloud provider. **Step 4:** Provider gives access to the spot instances.

Fig. 3.1 Combinatorial forward auction-based VM provisioning and allocation

this case, the provider allocates either complete bundle to the user or nothing. The assumption of single-minded bidders allows us to study the computational complexity and strategic behaviour in combinatorial auction in a more concrete manner. In Fig. 3.1, a basic framework of combinatorial forward auction-based Cloud market is given.

3.3.1 Combinatorial Forward Auction in Cloud Computing

In the Cloud market, Cloud users are the resource buyers who compete with each other by bidding in the market. Cloud provider is the seller who provides resources to the buyers based on their submitted bid [118, 175]. Among all the forward auction-based mechanisms, combinatorial auctions are the most studied mechanisms in Cloud computing. Therefore, the focus in this chapter is only on combinatorial auction. There are several reported works proposing combinatorial auction-based resource allocation and pricing mechanisms in Cloud computing. Several features make the combinatorial auction more promising and suitable to apply in the Cloud market. The Cloud resources are heterogeneous with some properties of complementarity and substitutability. A Cloud user executes various types of tasks/jobs which require different types of resources (VMs as the Cloud resources) with different configurations. For example, a user deploying a Web application needs three different types of resources for three different layers—storage intensive for Databases, compute intensive for middle-tier and memory intensive for front-end application layer [184]. Similarly, different types of services with different resource requirements (VMs with different configurations) are needed for building workflow applications on platform as a service (PaaS). PaaS, in this case, will act as a user and IaaS as a Cloud service provider. Combinatorial forward auction fits well to handle these kinds of situations.

3.4 VM Provisioning and Pricing in Cloud Market: A Combinatorial Auction-Based Formulation

VM Provisioning and pricing problem in Cloud market is a significant and important problem. The whole problem can be divided into two parts as follows:

Allocation and Provisioning Problem

In the first part, Cloud provider finds the winning users by solving the winner determination problem which is an important but NP-hard problem in combinatorial auction [50, 189]. The allocation process should allocate different set of resources (VMs) to different users in such a way that each set is disjoint and the total allocated capacity does not exceed the available capacity at Cloud data centre [50].

Pricing Problem

In the second part, a Cloud provider calculates the payments to be made by all the winning users. The payment mechanism is designed to satisfy some economics properties. Here, losing users will pay nothing and winning users pay to the provider for utilizing the resources. The payments to be made depend upon the allocation results obtained by solving the allocation problem.

3.4.1 Problem Formulation

In this section, the formulation of VM allocation and pricing problem is discussed. The said problem can be formulated in two ways depending upon how the VMs are provisioned.

3.4.1.1 Static VM Provisioning and Pricing Formulation

Let us consider the basic model of combinatorial auction in Cloud computing. Suppose there are N Cloud users and a single Cloud provider, offering K different types

Table 3.1 Amazon EC2 standard instances types

Instance type	Small	Medium	Large	Ex-large
EC2 compute unit	1	2	4	8
Memory	1.7 GB	3.75 GB	7.5 GB	15 GB
Storage	160 GB	410 GB	850 GB	1690 GB
I/O performance	Moderate	Moderate	High	High

of VMs. $\mathcal{N} = \{1, 2, \ldots, N\}$ and $\mathcal{K} = \{1, 2, \ldots, K\}$ denote the set of users and VMs, respectively. These VMs are heterogeneous in terms of their resource configurations (CPU, memory, network, storage, etc.) and can be compared by assigning a weight to each types of VM, i.e. $W = (w_1, w_2, \cdots, w_K)$ and $w_k \geq 0, \forall k \in \mathcal{K}$ and $w_1 \leq w_2 \leq \ldots \leq w_K$. The values of these weights, for all types of VMs, are calculated using the amount of resources in VMs. This characterization models the heterogeneity of VM instances correctly in the Cloud system. As an example, Microsoft Azure provides four types of VMs, i.e. small, medium, large and extra-large. These VMs are different in terms of their resource configurations. A small type of VM consists of 1.6 GHz CPU, 1.75 GB memory, 225 GB storage; a medium-size VM consists of 2×1.6 GHz CPU, 3.5 GB memory, 490 GB storage; a large-size VM consists of 4×1.6 GHz CPU, 7 GB memory, 1 TB storage; and an extra-large size VM consists of 8×1.6 GHz CPU, 14 GB memory, 2 TB storage [112]. For simplicity, it is assumed that the number of cores decides the weight of a VM. Then, in this example, weight vector will be $W = (1, 2, 4, 8)$. Similarly, combination of different resource quantities can be considered for calculating the weights. Another real example is distinct types of VMs provided by Amazon EC2. Table 3.1 depicts different types of Cloud instances provided by Amazon EC2 [5].

In static provisioning, a Cloud provider has a fixed number of VMs instances which would not change with the change in users' requests. The vector $(L_1, L_2, \ldots, L_K)$ represents the available capacity of each type of VM. $M = \sum_{k=1}^{K} L_k$ denotes the total capacities available at a Cloud provider.

Cloud users have certain tasks or jobs which they wish to execute on Cloud resources (VMs). A Cloud user may have the requirements of one or set of VMs. Each user has some valuation for each set of VMs, i.e. $v_i(s_i)$ where v_i denotes the valuation in monetary terms and $s_i \subseteq M$ represents the set of VMs requested by the user i. $v_i(s_i)$ represents the valuation, one is ready to pay for the complete bundle s_i. More clearly, v can be defined as a real-valued function $v: s \rightarrow \mathbb{R}$ where $v_i(\varphi) = 0$ and $v_i(s_i) \leq v_i(M)$ for any $s_i \subseteq M$.

A Cloud user's bid vector can be represented as $Bid_i = (b_i, p_i)$. Here, b_i is the requested bundle, i.e. $b_i = (b_1^i, b_2^i, \ldots, b_K^i)$, b_k^i is the number of VMs of type k requested by ith user and p_i is the amount of money the user is ready to pay for the requested bundle of resources. For example, if Cloud providers provide four distinct types of VMs and user i requests 2 VMs of type 1, 3 VMs of type 2, 1 VM of type 3 and 6 VMs of type 4 and the bid value for these VMs is \$10, then this bid can be represented as follows: $Bid_i = (\langle 2, 3, 1, 6 \rangle, \$10)$. Let pay_i is the payment done by the ith user. The utility of a user, i.e. $\mathcal{U}_i$, can be calculated as the difference between the actual valuation and the price one is paying, i.e. $\mathcal{U}_i = v_i(b_i) - pay_i$. A losing user's utility will always be zero.

The main goal of the VM provisioning and pricing problem is to maximize total social welfare while satisfying the resource availability constraint and some economic properties. The total social welfare will be the sum of all the valuations of the winning users. The social welfare maximization problem $\Pi(\mathcal{N}, v, b, L_k)$ can be formulated as an Integer Linear Programming (ILP) problem as in Eq. (3.1).

$$\Pi(\mathcal{N}, v, b, L_k): \text{maximize} SW(\mathcal{N}, v, b, L_k) = \sum_{i=1}^{N} v_i(b_i).x_i \qquad (3.1)$$

subject to

$$\sum_{i=1}^{N} x_i b_k^i \leq L_k \quad \forall k \in \mathcal{K} \qquad (3.2)$$

$$x_i \in \{0, 1\} \quad \forall i \in \mathcal{N} \qquad (3.3)$$

$$0 \leq pay_i \leq p_i \qquad (3.4)$$

In Eq. (3.1), $SW(\mathcal{N}, v, b, L_k)$ is the total social welfare that should be maximized. Equation (3.2) denotes that the allocated quantity of VMs should not exceed the available capacity for each type of VMs. Equation (3.3) depicts that decision variable x_i should be integer, the value of which is decided as follows.

$$x_l = \begin{cases} 1, & \text{if } b_i \text{ is allocated to user } i \\ 0, & \text{otherwise} \end{cases}$$

Equation (3.4) denotes the individual rationality constraint and ensures that a user's payment is always less than its valuation; i.e., the user is not at loss by participating in the auction.

To find the allocation vector, i.e. $(x_1, x_2, \ldots, x_N)$ for the above-said problem is called winner determination problem in combinatorial auction. It is an ILP-based combinatorial optimization NP-hard problem. The allocation process allocates the distinct set of VMs to the different users in such a way that each set is disjoint and the total allocated capacity does not exceed the available capacity.

Design Target and Objectives

In combinatorial auction where bidders bid for the bundles of resources, economic efficiency (with maximum social welfare) and computational efficiency (implementable in polynomial time) conflict with each other [50]. Of all the discussed properties, truthfulness is an important requirement. In this chapter, the focus is only on designing efficient and truthful combinatorial auction mechanisms. The said problem is solved keeping in mind the economic properties one should satisfy.

Economic Efficiency

Economic efficiency of an auction mechanism is measured in terms of total social welfare generated by the mechanism. An efficient mechanism maximizes the total social welfare. An auction mechanism is 100% efficient if the actual welfare generated by the mechanism is equal to the welfare generated theoretically; i.e., there is no loss of welfare in the mechanism.

Computational Efficiency

An auction mechanism is said to be computationally tractable if the allocation and payments can be determined in polynomial time.

Incentive Compatibility or Truthfulness

A truthful combinatorial auction mechanism ensures that bidding its true information is a dominant strategy for each user; i.e., for each i, $\mathcal{U}_i(\overline{p_i}) \geq \mathcal{U}_i(p_i) \forall i \in \mathcal{N}$ where $\mathcal{U}_i$ is the utility of user i, $\overline{p_i}$ and p_i are the actual and quoted valuation/price of ith user, respectively.

Individual Rational

An auction mechanism is said to be individual rational if utility of all the participants is always nonnegative; i.e., a user does not pay more than bid valuation, i.e. $\mathcal{U}_i \geq 0 \ \forall i \in \mathcal{N}$.

3.4.1.2 Dynamic VM Provisioning and Pricing Problem Formulation

In this case, all basic assumptions, design targets and objectives are same as in the static provisioning formulation discussed in above section except the way in which VMs are provisioned. Rather than fixing the quantity of each type of VMs as in static provisioning case, in this, it is assumed that VM of distinct types can be dynamically provisioned from the available resource pools after receiving the users' requests. The decision on which type of VMs and what quantity of VMs should be provisioned depends upon the users' requested data. Let there are C types of resources, i.e. CPU, memory, storage and $C = \{1, 2, \ldots, C\}$. Each type of VM consists of different amount of resources denoted by r_{kc} where k and c denote the VM type and resource type, respectively. It is assumed that the provider has fixed amount of each type of resources, i.e. L_c available for allocation. From Table 3.1, it is found that $r_{32} = 7.5$, $r_{23} = 410$, and so on. Dynamic provisioning helps a provider to increase its revenue by increasing the utilization of the resources. Let $d_c^i = \sum_{k=1}^{K} b_k^i r_{kc}$ is the total amount of resource of type c requested by the ith user.

Here also, the provider selects the users in such a way that the social welfare SW is maximized. This can be achieved by allocating the resources to those users who value them the most. The social welfare maximization problem $\Pi(\mathcal{N}, v, b, L_c)$ can be formulated as an Integer Linear Programming (ILP) problem as in Eq. (3.5).

$$\Pi(\mathcal{N}, v, b, L_c): \text{maximize } SW(\mathcal{N}, v, b, L_c) = \sum_{i=1}^{N} v_i(b_i).x_i \qquad (3.5)$$

subject to

$$\sum_{i=1}^{N} x_i d_c^i \leq L_c \quad \forall c \in \mathcal{C} \qquad (3.6)$$

$$x_i \in \{0, 1\} \quad \forall i \in \mathcal{N} \qquad (3.7)$$

$$0 \leq \text{pay}_i \leq p_i \qquad (3.8)$$

In the above formulation, in Eq. (3.5), $SW(\mathcal{N}, v, b, L_c)$ is the total social welfare that should be maximized. Equation (3.6) denotes that the allocated resource of each type should not exceed the available capacity for that type of resource. Equation (3.7) denotes the binary decision variable x_i and ensures that if a user wins, complete bundle is allocated; otherwise, users gets zero utility, i.e.

$$x_i = \begin{cases} 1, & \text{if } b_i \text{ is allocated to user } i \\ 0, & \text{otherwise} \end{cases}$$

Equation (3.8) denotes the individual rationality constraint which ensures that a user's payment is always less than its valuations.

3.4.2   Allocation Methods and Pricing Schemes

VM allocation and pricing problem satisfying certain economic properties is solved as discussed above. As pricing phase depends upon the results of allocation phase, both allocation methods and pricing schemes are discussed at one place that gives a unified view to the solution approaches of VM provisioning and pricing problem.

As winner determination problem is an NP-hard problem, to find the optimal allocation is computationally intractable, and therefore, heuristics are often applied for the same. The payment schemes are then designed accordingly for these allocation methods. If the social welfare maximization problem is solved in an optimal way, then VCG payment mechanism is used for truthful payments (VCG mechanisms are truthful only when the allocation results are optimal). For greedy approaches, payment schemes are modified according to allocation method for achieving the truthfulness. Also, bid on a bundle rather than on a single item makes it further challenging. Both computational efficiency and incentive compatibility cannot be achieved simultaneously in combinatorial auction. For this, we use some heuristic or approximation allocation schemes and design the payment scheme accordingly such that truthfulness is the dominant strategy for all the players. Users are selfish and strategic in nature. They want to maximize their utilities and can manipulate the market by bidding untruthfully; i.e., they can bid much lower or higher than their actual valuations which not only harm other users but also incur loss to the provider. So, the revenue of a Cloud provider cannot be maximized until the truthfulness is enforced into the auction mechanism. There are several ways to enforce strategy-proofness into the mechanism. One way is to implement dominant strategy incentive-compatible mechanism in which being truthful is the dominant strategy for each user; i.e., its utility will be maximum if bid truthfully.

3.4.2.1   Greedy Allocation and Proportional Critical Value Pricing

An approximated, efficient and truthful mechanism is proposed in [93] with the greedy allocation schemes along with proportional critical value pricing scheme by modifying the standard GVA [84] mechanisms. The authors considered the critical payment concept and the bid density as a norm for calculating the payments of winning bidders. The proposed scheme is as follows.

Allocation Scheme

Greedy method is used for allocating the items/goods among the bidders. First all the bidders are sorted according to their bid densities after which the requested items are allocated to the bidders one by one.

Proportional Value Pricing

There are two cases:

- If a bidder loses, then she pays nothing or zero.
- If a bidder wins, then she pays to the provider according to the critical value pricing scheme. For each bidder i, select a bidder j who would be the winner if bidder i does not participate in auction. Calculate the payment of bidder i by multiplying the bid density of bidder j with the bundle size of bidder i.

The proposed mechanism, in the above work, is approximately efficient and truthful. They proved this by showing the proof for all the four properties viz. exactness, monotonicity, critical payment and participation as discussed in Sect. 3.3.1. The authors also studied the case of complex bidders that are not single-minded. They showed that for complex bidders or non-single-minded bidders with greedy allocation schemes, there do not exist any pricing schemes which make the mechanism truthful.

Reference [209] extended the mechanism proposed in [93], and [8] proposed the combinatorial auction-based models for VM allocation in Cloud computing. The work assumes that VMs available at the Cloud provider side are of heterogeneous nature; i.e., they are different in their resource configurations like CPU, memory, storage, network. They considered the static provisioning of the VM resources; i.e., a Cloud provider has fixed number of VM instances that are provisioned in advance in auction-based market. The authors proposed two combinatorial auction-based mechanisms *CA-LP* and *CA-GREEDY* to allocate the VM instances among the Cloud users to maximize the total social welfare in the Cloud market. A combinatorial auction-based mechanism is proposed in [8] with the assumption that number of each type of items cannot be greater than one. The first mechanism *CA-LP* extends the mechanism of [8] by relaxing this constraint and considering the combinatorial auction where bids are in the form of bundles. The *CA-LP* mechanism solves the VM allocation problem using the linear programming (LP) relaxation and randomized rounding. Authors claimed that the proposed mechanism achieves truthfulness in expectation. The second mechanism, proposed in this work, i.e. *CA-GREEDY*, is the extension of the mechanism proposed in [93] which gives the approximated solutions with an approximation ratio of $\sqrt{M}$ where M is the weighted total number of requested resources, i.e. $M = \sum_{i=1}^{m} w_i k_i$. Here, w_i and k_i are the weight of the ith VM and total number of ith type of VMs available, respectively.

The mechanism first sorts the bidders according to their bid densities. After this, it allocates the VMs one by one to the top bidders in the sorted list. The allocation continues until the whole capacity is not exhausted. The payment scheme, based on critical payment, is modified according to the greedy allocation scheme. The payment for each winning user u_i depends upon the bid value of the losing bidder who would win if u_i did not participate in auction. If there are more than one losing bidders, then bidder with the highest bid density is chosen among all the losing bidders. The basic difference between the works of [93, 209] is in the calculation of the bid density. Reference [209] considers the weighted average of all VM instance types which is more suitable in Cloud scenario and approximated the allocation results with approximation ratio of $\sqrt{M}$.

These two mechanisms were compared with fixed-price mechanism through simulation on parameters such as generated revenue, resource utilization and allocation efficiency. The experimental results show the effectiveness of the proposed mechanism over the fixed-price mechanisms. Running time of *CA–LP* is more than other mechanisms due to its iterative payment mechanism. Although *CA–LP* is effective for generating more revenue and higher resource utilization, still *CA–LP* cannot be used in case of large number of users due to higher computational complexity. *CA–GREEDY* performs well in all environments and overall most preferable among all three mechanisms for the VM allocation problem. However, certain things such as dynamic provisioning of the VM resources, reserve price are not considered in the work.

Same authors, in their extended work in [208], addressed the static provisioning issue by proposing combinatorial auction-based models for dynamic VM provisioning. Their model was different from [209] in the way the VMs are provisioned and allocated. [209] considers the static VM provisioning, while *CA-PROVISION* proposed in [208] considers the reserve price and dynamic provisioning of VM resources. The main objective, considered in the work, is to maximize the profit of the Cloud provider. It also considers the running and idle cost of VMs for provider's benefit. The profit of a Cloud provider is the sum of payments done by the winning users minus the total cost incurred due to VM instances. This total cost is the sum of cost due to running instances as well as idle instances. *CA–PROVISION* achieved higher utilization as compared to the static provisioning model proposed in [209]. Extensive simulation experiments were performed on real workload to evaluate the effectiveness of the model. *CA–PROVISION* performs better than *CA–GREEDY* on higher revenue, resource utilization and percentage of served users. However, in high-demand case, *CA–GREEDY* generates more profit to the Cloud provider as compared to the *CA–PROVISION*.

In [132], a family of truthful combinatorial auction mechanisms for VM provisioning and allocation problem for Cloud computing (VMPAC) has been designed. The mechanisms were based on the greedy heuristics and consider the heterogeneity of VM resources and users' demand. Dynamic provisioning of the VM resources is considered in VMPAC which provides approximated results while satisfying the truthfulness property for an arbitrary number of bidders. The payments, for the resources, were based on the critical payment methods as proposed in [93] and [209]. Three algorithms, presented in [132], are described as follows.

- *G-VMPAC-I-ALLOC*: This mechanism is a direct generalization of the work in [93] and does not consider the heterogeneity of the resources. This mechanism is preferable only when the resources are homogeneous and therefore not suitable for the Cloud environment.
- *G-VMPAC-II-ALLOC*: This mechanism considers the resource scarcity aspect. Priority of the users will depend upon their bid value and the availability of the resources for which they are bidding. This mechanism considers heterogeneous demands of resources from users. If a user is demanding a scarce resource, its chance of winning decreases and vice versa.
- *G-VMPAC-III-ALLOC*: This mechanism considers the relative and not the absolute scarcity of the resources. A user, bidding for less demanded resources, has better chance to win as compared to the case where it bids for highly demanded resources.

All three mechanisms are truthful and approximately efficient with an approximation ratio of $\sqrt{N}RC_{max}$ where N is the number of Cloud users; R is the total resource types; and C_{max} is the maximum capacity of a resource available with the Cloud provider.

The simulation experiments were performed on a real Grid workload and depict that it performs better than the competing mechanisms. All mechanisms, besides optimal and CA–PROVISION mechanisms, were compared with each other in terms of average social welfare, total revenue generated and utilization of the resources. Among all mechanisms, the optimal mechanism gives the optimal results for revenue and social welfare though with higher execution time. For large number of bidders, it cannot be executed in polynomial time. G-VMPAC-II-ALLOC performs better than all other greedy-based mechanisms and produces results quickly.

3.4.2.2   Approximation-Based Allocation and Critical Payment

Approximation algorithms give sub-optimal and bounded solution for NP-hard problems and their margin to optimality can be quantified using the *"approximation ratio"* associated with an approximation algorithm. However, most of these algorithms cannot be used for designing truthful mechanisms. The reason being the monotonicity property is not satisfied by these algorithms. Monotonicity is a necessary condition for a truthful mechanism [30, 93]. For example, randomized rounding technique for solving packing integer programming (PIP) problems is not monotonic [30].

However, there are some polynomial time approximation schemes (PTAS) algorithms which are monotonic and suitable for designing truthful and approximately efficient mechanisms. For PTAS-based allocation algorithms, proposed in [30, 106], truthful payments are calculated using critical value concept [93]. In this, critical values for each user can be found using binary search method. Reference [106] considered the basic model proposed in [132] and designed the PTAS for the VM allocation problem. A PTAS scheme is ε—approximation algorithm that produces results within $(1 - \varepsilon)$ of the optimal result where $0 < \varepsilon < 1$. The results presented in [106] claimed the strongest approximation results for the VM provisioning problem. The proposed mechanism also considered the system heterogeneity and dynamic provisioning of VM resources. In the work, *PTAS-VMPAC* mechanism was proposed which consists of two methods called *PTAS-ALLOC* and *C-PAY*. *PTAS-ALLOC* scheme is based on the work in [30] which proposed a truthful approximated allocation algorithm for general assignment problem. The accuracy of the solution is controlled by a parameter q where $q \leq N$ where N is the total number of Cloud users. As the value of q increases, better solution is obtained though at the cost of increase in computation time. When $q=N$, the algorithm converts to brute-force approach and execution becomes computationally intractable. The payment scheme *C–PAY* is based on critical payment, and binary search is used to find the critical payment for each user. The mechanism *PTAS-VMPAC* is truthful because *PTAS-ALLOC* is monotone and *C-PAY* is based on critical payment [93]. The three mechanisms *VCG-VMPAC*, *PTAS-VMPAC* and *G-VMPAC-II-ALLOC* [131] were compared with each other experimentally on real grid workload. The quality of the solution produced by *PTAS-VMPAC* depends upon the available capacity and total size of the user's requests. It is shown that *PTAS-VMPAC* achieves similar results to that of optimal mechanism *VCG-VMPAC* on all workload logs for $\varepsilon = 0.5$. Also, the number of served users is same in both the mechanisms. The results showed that *PTAS-VMPAC* generates near-optimal results and its execution time depends upon the number of users and ε. However, the experiments were performed on the grid workload and do not consider the Cloud environment.

3.4.2.3   OPTIMAL Allocation and VCG Mechanisms

There are several methods like dynamic programming, branch-and-bound, brute-force in which optimal solutions for VM allocation can be achieved, but only some

Table 3.2 Comparison of auction-based VM allocation methods in Cloud computing

Reference	Heterogeneous VMs	Incentive compatible	Optimal	Computation time	Provisioning type
[93]	No	Yes	No	Less	Static
[209]	Yes	Yes, truthful in expectation	No	Less	Static
[208]	Yes	Yes	Yes	High	Dynamic
[132]	Yes	Yes	No	Less	Dynamic
[106]	Yes	Yes	Yes	High	Dynamic

of these techniques can be used for designing truthful mechanisms. The drawbacks of the above mechanisms were the amount of time they take in execution and hence not suitable for large market size where number of Cloud users are large. In [106], truthful optimal mechanism *VCG-VMPAC* was proposed in which the winner determination problem is solved using the dynamic programming-based approach *DP–VMPAC*. Along with, VCG payments scheme, *VCG–PAY* is used for user's payments. The optimal mechanisms were based on the VCG payment though not implementable for large number of bidders due to their higher computational complexity.

Table 3.2 presents a comparative study of VM provisioning methods proposed in Cloud computing.

3.5 Issues and Challenges

Although Amazon offers its unutilized capacity to its users using spot pricing and this way of offering instances is very successful till date, there are various issues and research gaps that need proper attention by the researchers of these discipline. This section elaborates some issues and research challenges regarding the implantation of combinatorial auction-based mechanisms.

3.5.1 Designing Efficient and Truthful Mechanisms

Computational complexity is the main issue for a combinatorial auction. Designing revenue-maximizing combinatorial auction is a well-recognized and open problem in mechanism design. It is unsolved even for two bidders and two sale items. However, [109] found that complex auction mechanism such as combinatorial auction mechanisms were not adopted for spectrum license allocation due to their implementation intractability as finding the winning bidders in combinatorial auction is a NP-hard problem. Therefore, Federal Communications Commission (FCC) adopted another kind of auction called Simultaneously Ascending Auction (SAA) [116, 154].

In combinatorial auction, the main goal of the mechanism is to maximize the social welfare (the sum of valuations of all bidders). However, VCG payment schemes [45, 67, 186] cannot be used (although they are allocative efficient and truthful by nature) for combinatorial auction as they are computationally inefficient. More specifically, VCG mechanism exhibits the property of incentive compatible only if the allocation is optimal [93]. Allocative efficiency and incentive compatibility can be achieved by simply applying VCG mechanisms, but computational efficiency gets compromised. However, exact or optimal solution of winner determination problem in combinatorial auction is computationally intractable [159]. Moreover, the VCG mechanism has many issues such as winner determination effort, revenue deficiency, budget constraints, weak equilibrium that makes it impractical in a real market [155].

In the domain of combinatorial auction, designing a mechanism that is both allocative efficient and incentive compatible is a major research problem. The winner determination problem or the social welfare maximization problem in combinatorial auction is an NP-hard problem. This above problem exists only for multidimensional problems, e.g. combinatorial auction [88]. In single-dimensional case, the requirement of truthfulness simply reduces to the algorithmic monotonic condition. The work proposed in [13] shows that winner determination problem or social welfare maximization problem in simple combinatorial exchange cannot be approximated even with free disposal constraint. Therefore, in this case, heuristics or approximation techniques seem quite reasonable in the auction design. These techniques are highly scalable and produces near-optimal results as compared to the exact mechanisms which give the optimal results to the allocation problem but infeasible in implementation. Some algorithmic techniques, such as greedy methods, are quite useful when used in the auction context and more specifically when the auction is repetitive. The reason for the above argument is that in repetitive auction system, solution is required in very limited time and approximation and heuristics methods exhibit very less computational complexity. Both the allocation and payment functions are to be computed in reasonable time in these types of auction. In this case, we must modify the truthful pricing mechanisms (e.g. VCG, Clarke's, second-price mechanism) according to the allocation function so that truthfulness property remains in the mechanism.

3.5.2 Practical Combinatorial Auction-Based Mechanisms: Implementation in Real Cloud

VM provisioning and pricing mechanism should be viewed from both the economic and computational points of view. From economics point of view, it is a *Design problem* which is more concerned about economic properties such as truthfulness, individual rationality in a Cloud market. The computational perspective focuses on the *Implementation problem* which finds whether the designed combinatorial auction mechanism is implemented in polynomial time as the corresponding optimization problem is NP-hard. In Cloud market, both user and provider want simple and fast mechanisms which provision the Cloud resources in a reasonable amount of time. Further, these mechanisms should allow all the participants to communicate with each other with the least complexity. Designing a combinatorial auction-based resource allocation and pricing mechanism, which considers the solution of both the above problems, is very complex and is a potential topic for future research.

3.5.3 Bidding Strategies Designing

Bidding strategy of a user depends on numerous factors such as variable workload and deadline constraints, urgency of a job, number of providers, checkpointing techniques, alternative SLAs. Several research challenges, involved in bidding strategy design, are as follows.

- While designing bidding strategy for users, a natural question arises as how bidders' strategy would affect the providers' behaviour in the spot market. Therefore, the perspective of provider in determining the spot prices by observing the strategic bidding behaviour of bidders could be another potential area for future research [213].
- Designing of bidding strategies in the presence of different types of bidders (irrational, risk-neutral, risk averse, etc.) [139] could also be a promising future research area.
- In the process of designing bidding strategy, most of the works consider the identical jobs/tasks. Designing a general bidding strategy which includes the heterogeneity of jobs/tasks and users can further be a good research topic. Also, there is a need for incorporating risk-awareness into users' bidding behaviour [210].

3.5.4 Bundling

In combinatorial auction, resources are allocated to those users who value them most in order to generate maximum revenue and maximize the economic efficiency. Before the allocation, users face a difficult problem of determining the optimal combination of resources that they should bid in order to get the maximum utility. This problem is an optimization problem with various parameters such as size of bundle, type of VMs, number of each type of VMs, required QoS, users' budget and most importantly finding the valuation of that bundle [65, 153]. This decision is multidimensional and requires understanding of auction dynamics, past experience and accurate knowledge of Cloud market [37, 187]. A user can learn from its winning history and accordingly can select optimal combination of resources for bidding. A bidder's decision-making would depend on its winning/losing bundle, its risk and its attitude towards market [130].

3.6 Summary

This chapter focuses on the combinatorial forward auction-based resource allocation and pricing mechanisms in the Cloud market. Fundamentals of combinatorial auction are discussed with desired goal and objectives. In addition, truthfulness in combinatorial auction is explicitly discussed. A basic framework of combinatorial auction is presented in order to understand the basic steps in designing the real implementation of the forward auction. The applicability of the combinatorial forward auction in Cloud has been explicitly discussed. All the major combinatorial auction-based models in Cloud computing have been analysed and compared in terms of various auction properties. VM provisioning and pricing problem is formulated, from both the static and dynamic points of view, which gives an idea of how to formulate the basic allocation and pricing problem in a Cloud market. Several issues, identified during the literature survey, are deliberated along with the challenges that need to be addressed in future.

As Amazon spot market is the only real implementation of forward auction-based mechanisms, it is a great opportunity for the research community (industry as well as academia) to design other efficient, sustainable and viable forward auction-based Cloud market mechanisms for resource provisioning. This chapter intends to encourage the researchers to design alternatives of Amazon spot market by resolving various discussed issues.

Chapter 4
Reverse Auction-Based Cloud Resource Provisioning

Abstract Out of many auction techniques, reverse auction is the one in which providers act as bidders. In this chapter, a detailed description of reverse auction and its benefits to Cloud providers and customers are discussed. Various attributes of reverse auction are presented in the Cloud scenario for its applicability. Various auction properties, an auction designer vies to achieve, have also been listed and deliberated. A detailed and comparative survey of existing works in reverse auction on the basis of auction properties is given to better understand the state of the art of reverse auction in Cloud. A truthful combinatorial reverse auction model is also presented to help in understanding and designing a reverse auction mechanism for the Cloud researchers in order to achieve a defined goal. Open research issues are highlighted to provide an insight for the future research work in this area.

4.1 Introduction

Two types of reverse auction, related to Cloud computing, are reported in the literature: single-unit single-item reverse auction and combinatorial reverse auction. In the former, customer prepares its call for proposal (CFP) containing single unit of single item and advertises the same in the Cloud market. The providers then prepare their offers in the form of a bid to compete with each other. In the latter, a bid is prepared considering a combination of various types of resources required by the customer. Usually, providers are reluctant to reveal the true value of their resources. This demands the auction designing in such a way that optimizes the pay-off of the providers when they reveal their true value. During the domain analysis, some works have been noticed that design a truthful single-unit single-item reverse auction. However, to the authors' best knowledge, no such models have been reported using combinatorial reverse auction.

The existing works in reverse auction foresee a better Cloud resource usage. It is not possible to predict the long-term effects of reverse auction in Cloud computing since there is no real working model for the Cloud resource usage. For example, it might be possible that economy surges and a tight supply market emerges [23]. In

© The Author(s) 2018
G. Baranwal et al., *Auction Based Resource Provisioning in Cloud Computing*,
SpringerBriefs in Computer Science, https://doi.org/10.1007/978-981-10-8737-0_4

that situation, customers are competitive in nature and providers may offer resources using forward auction. Therefore, this work also makes a close observation on reverse auction discussed and implemented in other domain as well. A detailed description on reverse auction in Cloud would help the readers to understand this topic clearly. Various proposed approaches, for resource allocation using reverse auction in the Cloud, have been summarized for better understanding of the work done in the recent past. A truthful combinatorial auction has been formulated and compared with baseline model in single-unit single-item reverse auction. Research gaps are also identified which directs the possible future research in Cloud computing.

The outline of this chapter is as follows. Section 4.2 gives the detailed description of reverse auction, its benefits to Cloud provider and Cloud customer, and description of various auction properties that an auction designer tries to achieve. Section 4.3 summarizes the existing reported works on reverse auction and compares them on the basis of various auction properties. Section 4.4 presents a scenario of the reverse auction-based Cloud market. A truthful combinatorial reverse auction is proposed and compared with baseline model in Sect. 4.5, while some open research issues in reverse auction have been identified in Sect. 4.6. Finally, Sect. 4.7 summarizes the chapter.

4.2 Reverse Auction

Reverse auction is a well-known game-theoretic mechanism for resource allocation applied in many disciplines. In its early stages, reverse auction did not receive much attention, but due to rapid growth in network technology, i.e. Internet and e-commerce over the past few decades, reverse auction is being implemented successfully in various business domains such as retail, electronics, IT, automotive, defence, petroleum [23, 35]. These developments led electronic reverse auction as an important tool for purchasing. Electronic reverse auction has been defined in [23] as "*An online, real-time dynamic auction between a buying organization and a group of pre-qualified suppliers who compete against each other to win the business to supply goods or services that have clearly defined specifications for design, quantity, quality, delivery, and related terms and conditions. These suppliers compete by bidding against each other online over the Internet using specialized software by submitting successively lower priced bids during a scheduled time period*".

4.2.1 Attributes of Reverse Auction

Various attributes, a business should have to conduct reverse auction, have been identified in [23]. This section lists these attributes while discussing its feasibility in the Cloud scenario.

Specified and Charged Service

In Cloud, VMs are the biddable items. The configuration of VMs can be clearly specified. The current literature states that QoS metrics, required for VMs, not only can be described but can be quantified as well [17, 19, 63]. Users can clearly specify its requirements too.

Strong Likelihood of High Offered Price

Due to a stiff competition among the providers in the growing Cloud market, a significant reduction in the cost of the Cloud services has been observed [12]. Business sense leads us to believe that a provider does not offer these services at a loss. Therefore, it is quite likely that the customers are not availing the Cloud services at a right market price but at a premium. Emiliani [54] suggested that reverse auction is best suited for those customers who do not understand the cost of the resources, thus making it quite useful in the Cloud scenario.

Less-Affected Buyers, i.e. Less Switching Cost

Cloud provides the services on demand. Users can fetch the services from any Cloud providers as per their convenience though vendor lock-in, preventing the switching of users from one service provider to another, is still a real challenge. That is why interoperability is an important issue for realizing seamless Cloud services. This demands an open standard that provides interoperability in Cloud. Cloud Computing Interoperability Forum (CCIF), DMTF Cloud Standards Incubator, Open Cloud Manifesto, etc., are some organizations that are working towards the realization of some open standards. Further, Open Virtualization Format (OVF) supported by few Cloud vendors already provides the facility to switch from one vendor to another.

Sufficient Number of Qualified Service Providers

Stiff competition among Cloud providers has resulted in an increased number of service providers. These providers intend to enhance their base to maximum customers for their sustainability and profits. CLOUDORADO [48] is a Web service that lists various providers (around 25) and their offerings for Cloud hosting. Through this, user can specify its requirement specification so that only those providers are eligible who satisfy the requirements of the user. It is observed that sufficient number of qualifying service providers is available in the Cloud market.

Qualified Service Providers Ready for Bidding

As discussed, reverse auction in Cloud is a futuristic scenario. The presence of sufficient number of Cloud providers, competitive market of Cloud and benefits of reverse auction offers a positive hope for the implementation of reverse auction with the providers ready to bid and flourish.

Thus, it can be observed that Cloud-based businesses possess all the attributes in order to apply reverse auction benefiting both the users and the service providers.

4.2.2 Properties of Reverse Auction

Various properties, related to auction, have been elaborated in the literature. A good auction design should ensure to possess maximum of these properties. Mechanism design is very helpful in auction design with the desired objectives [127]. Various auction properties, for reverse auction, are as follows.

Incentive Compatibility

Reverse auction is called incentive compatible, strategy proof or truthful when all the providers get highest utility on honest bidding. This means that the pay-off of a provider is maximum when the provider reveals its true information [127].

Individual Rationality

Reverse auction is individual rational when the provider's utility or pay-off is always greater than or equal to zero. When a provider participates in an auction, it should never get a negative utility [127].

Buyer Optimality

Buyer optimality means customer gets the resources at the best available price. But to ensure incentive compatibility, customer has to give some incentives in terms of the money to the providers for revealing their true information. That is why when a reverse auction is designed to ensure incentive compatibility, customer has to pay more than the best available price. For example, in second-pricing auction, customer pays the second lowest price to the lowest price bidder. In the literature, it has been proved that an auction mechanism cannot be both incentive compatible and buyer optimal [99].

Budget-balance

It means that the customer transfers all the money to the winning providers only and there is no third-party subvention in payment settlement. In other words, the sum of the money transferred to all the participants is zero [127].

Non-dominance

A uni-attribute auction, in which a bid contains only price, is considered efficient when best bid is provided by the winning bidder only [99]. In multi-attribute auction, where bid contains both price and non-price attributes, the term "efficient" is named as non-dominant. A multi-attribute auction is said to be non-dominant when non-dominated bid is provided by only the winning bidder [99].

4.2.3 Benefits of Reverse Auction

Cloud market is a growing one resulting in huge competition among the service providers. Reverse auction has been proven to be beneficial to not only the customers but also the service providers. Benefits of reverse auction for both customers and providers are as follows.

4.2.3.1   To Cloud Customers

The benefits of reverse auction to Cloud customers are as follows.

Providers have Greater Responsibility: Selection of the most suitable Cloud provider is increasingly getting difficult because of the availability of the large number of service providers. But in reverse auction the customer is only required to prepare the call for proposal (CFP), while most of other work is done by the providers. After the acceptance of the bids from the providers, the auctioneer only needs to select the best provider as per the user's requirements. Instead of customer choosing the provider, providers compete to provide the resources or the services to the user.

Cost Reduction: Since bids are submitted by all suitable providers, who compete to win, providers are bound to offer the resources at the minimum possible or the best price. In reverse auction, the probability of availing resources at right market price by the customer is high. Therefore, reverse auction helps to reduce the procurement cost.

Time Saving: As mentioned earlier, customers need to specify their requirements in their CFP. This saves their time to check every provider and their services in order to select the best one. Probability of best matching of requirements of customer by the offerings of the provider also becomes high using reverse auction.

Efficient: Reverse auction is an efficient method to fetch the resources at the best price. It might be possible that cost saving in early stage of the auction is more but decreases with time [102]. Though some work suggests that exploration of efficiency from resulting productivity gains, innovation, integration, bundling, etc., are some factors that may be helpful in continuous saving [165], in any case, customer will get the resources at the best price or close to best price in an efficient manner.

Improved Customer–Provider Relationship: Reverse auction forces the customer and the provider to clearly specify their requirements and offers, respectively. Customers get the resources at minimum price in an efficient manner, while market cost of the providers also reduces in the process. This results in an improved relationship between the customers and the providers.

4.2.3.2   To Cloud Providers

The benefits of reverse auction to Cloud providers are as follows.

Fair Opportunity: New providers get competitive markets for their services. Monopolies of incumbent suppliers are reduced, and new providers, with the capability to satisfy the needs of the customers, get a fair chance to win the auction.

Market Exploration: Qualified providers get invitation for participation in future auction from existing as well as new customers on the basis of the market feedback. Therefore, reverse auction reduces the marketing and sale cost of the providers.

Current Market Understanding: Feedbacks, obtained from the customers, help providers to understand the current market scenario and to validate their competitiveness. This improves their bidding strategy.

Increased Resource Utilization: A provider gets more chances to participate in many auctions, and providers' winning in many rounds will increase the utilization of the resources.

4.3   Related Work on Reverse Auction in Cloud

Reverse auction has been applied earlier in grid computing for the resource allocation problem [78, 98]. In [78], two parameters are considered to define the pay-off of the customer, job completion time and minimum reliability threshold. Minimum reliability threshold calculates the frequency of completion of jobs before a deadline by the provider. It proposes a decentralized reverse auction which is truthful and dynamic in nature in which providers bid and one which maximizes the pay-off of the customer wins the auction. Providers bid to fulfil the need of the user, defined on the basis of task deadline and budget in [98]. A provider with the lowest bid, i.e. cheapest price, wins the auction. Experimental study, in [98], indicates that auction-based resource allocation is better in comparison with commodity market in grid computing in terms of completion time of jobs, user's utility, load balancing and societal utility.

In [173], a combinatorial reverse auction is proposed in which more than one bidder form a coalition on the basis of some mutual business relationships. Though authors considered QoS as an important factor in the proposed auction, they do not provide the details on how QoS is contributing in the winner determination.

In [82], authors have mentioned the idea about resource donation in a decentralized distributed Cloud environment; i.e., if a user donates its resource, it can use the resources donated by the other users. Resource discovery and resource allocation are the two issues addressed by the authors. For resource discovery, a multi-valued distributed hash table is used, whereas for resource allocation auction is used. In the auction, a reserve bid is defined by the user and bid closer to this reserve bid wins the auction. Participation of the users, in the donation of the resources, also plays an important role in the winner determination. Although, no experimental details have been provided to show the effectiveness or the efficiency of the proposed work.

The concept that allocation of the spare resources increases the revenue, a reverse auction mechanism is proposed in [120] by implementing this. In this mechanism, types of VM, length of task and revenue of the provider are also considered other than utilization of the spare resources to define the strategy of the providers which can be random or adaptive. A provider may not win all auctions in which it participates. Accordingly, the provider may not be able to achieve maximum utilization of the resources. To resolve this, [27] considered a mechanism of overbooking in auction [176]. Overbooking here implies that the providers compete for more customer demand than it may eventually serve. The problem with overbooking is that

providers may overuse it for their own benefits. To prevent this, authors in [27] introduced the concept of penalty on the provider. It is shown, through experiments, that
tuning of parameters for designing strategy for providers, i.e. adaptive strategy, can
lead to achieve business objectives while overbooking gives a chance to the provider
for maximal resource utilization.

Procurement of e-auction for service selection based on matching and ranking
algorithm is proposed in [7]. It improved the truthfulness by encouraging trustworthy bids. Since the functional and non-functional requirements of customer cannot
be ignored, the work suggests integrating these attributes within the SLA contract.
However, the work considered only non-functional requirements in the proposed
work and categorized them in security (e.g. integrity, confidentiality), performance
(e.g. response time, throughput) and dependability (e.g. reliability, availability). SLA
templates, considering non-functional requirements, can be used to match the requirements of the customer. A priority, attached with each attribute, helps in ordering of
the selected providers during matching process. Experimental study suggests that
the overhead of prototype of auction in terms of matching time and execution time
is acceptable in real time even in the worst case and its performance is comparable
to query-based selection engine.

A mechanism based on reverse auction for dynamic scheduling of workflows
in multi-Cloud environment is designed in [58]. In this, a multi-objective workflow scheduling class problem is considered. Two objectives, for optimization, are
makespan and monetary cost. Providers are assumed as selfish and non-cooperative
and have private information. Authors first designed a truthful mechanism for
scheduling of single task using VCG pricing scheme. They also imposed penalty,
on the provider, if it is not able to deliver the promised service. This mechanism is
a tailored mechanism for scheduling of the dynamic workflow, and the theoretical
investigation is not possible. Pareto optimal non-dominated solutions are generated.
The experimental analysis of the proposed model establishes that the obtained solutions are approximately Pareto optimal and have better coverage in comparison with
well-known multi-objective evolutionary algorithms SPEA2 and NSGAII [207].

In [146], three reverse auction mechanisms are proposed for a single item. The
first one is Cloud-dominant strategy incentive compatible (C-DSIC) which is allocative efficient and individual rational in nature but does not hold budget-balanced
property. The second mechanism is Cloud-Bayesian incentive compatible (C-BIC)
which is budget-balanced and allocative efficient in nature but does not hold the
individual rationality. The third is Cloud-optimal (C-OPT) which overcomes the
drawbacks of both the above-discussed mechanisms. User can choose any of these
mechanisms according to its requirements. Authors of [146] extended the work for
combinatorial reverse auction and used a variant of Combinatorial Auctions Branch
on Bids (CABOB) to decide the winner [162]. Experimental analysis suggests that
combinatorial auction is better in comparison with the sequential auction.

For optimal resource allocation, authors used immune evolutionary algorithm
in [195] considering three criteria, i.e. quality of service, efficiency of market and
satisfaction of the customer. Authors named this mechanism as reverse batch making auction (RBMA). Since malicious bidder can do some fraud and can affect the

decision-making about the price of the resource for both customer and provider, authors considered this aspect also and used a twice-punishment mechanism to prevent fraud behaviour of bidders. Authors proved the validity of the proposed work in terms of utilization of the resources and the efficiency of the market by the experimental analysis.

Winner determination problem of multi-item single-unit multi-attribute combinatorial reverse auction has been considered in [149]. A scenario of combinatorial reverse auction has been considered, but bundle contains only one unit of each item, i.e. single-unit multi-item reverse auction. Since non-price attributes must also play a role in deciding the winner, authors considered two objectives in the proposed work: first is minimization of payment by the customer, i.e. procurement cost, and another is maximization of score calculated by non-price attributes. This two-objective problem is converted into a single-objective problem by taking the preference of both the objectives by the user. Improved particle swarm optimization is proposed to find the solution, i.e. the winners of this single-objective problem. Though authors claim that the work proposed in [149] is a multi-attribute combinatorial reverse auction, few deficiencies in this work are noticeable. First, combinatorial auction is not limited to a single unit of each type of item in Cloud computing, and second, proposed auction mechanism focuses on allocation of the resources only where pricing plays major role in designing the mechanism. The proposed work in [149] is neither truthful nor it explains which auction properties it holds. Another issue is the imposition of penalty in the formulation of the problem in case services are not delivered on time. But the problem is non-price attributes, such as QoS, can be measured only after the delivery of the services. This raises the concern that the penalty should be considered after the allocation of the resources and not before the allocation.

4.3.1 Comparative Study Based on Auction Properties

Through the literature survey, it has been observed that only few works clearly mention the auction properties. A comparative representation of some existing works, on these properties, has been summarized in Table 4.1.

4.4 Framework for Cloud Market Using Reverse Auction

In reverse auction-based Cloud market, three active entities are Cloud customer, Cloud provider and Cloud auctioneer. A Cloud customer needs resources to execute its tasks by identifying its requirement and submitting it to the Cloud auctioneer. Cloud auctioneer converts customer's requirement into CFP and publishes it into the Cloud market. After accepting the bids, from the providers, auctioneer decides the winner. This section provides a glimpse of auction-based Cloud market and provides the details of all three active entities.

Table 4.1 Comparison of reverse auction-based models in Cloud computing

Model/references	Auction properties						
	CA	MA	IC	BO	ND	IR	BB
[98]	✗	✓	✗	✓	✓	✓	–
[173]	✓	✓	✗	✓	✓	✓	✓
[27]	✓	✗	✗	✓	✓	✓	–
[146]	✗	✓	✓	✗	✗	✓	✓
[147]	✓	✓	✗	✓	–	✓	✓

CA combinatorial auction; *MA* multi-attribute; *IC* incentive compatible; *BO* buyer's optimality; *ND* non-dominance; *IR* individual rationality; *BB* budget-balance

Cloud Customer

Cloud customer or Cloud user needs services or computing resources to execute the tasks. The customer identifies the requirement in terms of computing resources and QoS expectation and submits it to the auctioneer.

Cloud Auctioneer

Cloud customer can run the auction itself or may contact to a Cloud auctioneer for running the auction on his/her behalf. After receiving the requirement from the customer, auctioneer prepares a call for proposal, i.e. CFP, and publishes it in the market to accept the bids from the Cloud providers. After receiving the bids from the providers, auctioneer runs a winner determination algorithm and informs the providers about the winners.

Cloud Providers

Cloud providers offer the computing resources to the customers on the payment basis. After receiving the CFP from the auctioneer, providers prepare their bid accordingly. During the formation of bundle, providers may even offer only one resource. Here, it is assumed that providers are single-minded bidders; i.e., they will allocate the whole bundle or nothing. Provider needs to allocate the mentioned resources in the bundle to the customer if it wins the auction.

Sequence diagram of the reverse auction is given in Fig. 4.1, and the steps involved are given in the following box.

0. Begin
1. Cloud Customer submits requirements to Cloud Auctioneer.
2. Cloud Auctioneer starts auction.
3. Cloud Auctioneer publishes requirements and informs Cloud Providers about the starting of auction.
4. Cloud Providers submit their bids to Cloud Auctioneer.
5. Cloud Auctioneer acknowledges Cloud Providers about their bids.

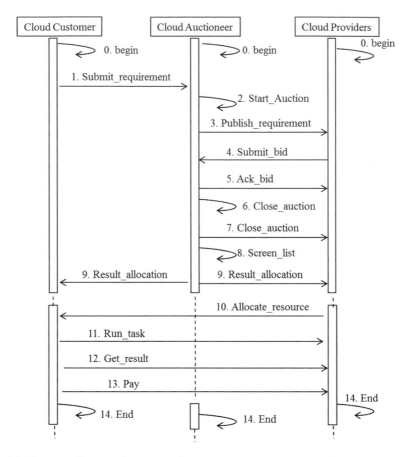

Fig. 4.1 Sequence diagram of reverse auction

6.   Cloud Auctioneer closes the auction.
7.   Cloud Auctioneer informs Cloud Providers about closing of auction.
8.   Cloud Auctioneer screens initial list of bids.
9.   Cloud Auctioneer solves winner determination problem and sends obtained result, i.e. result of allocation of resources to Cloud Customer and Cloud Providers.
10. Cloud Providers allocate the resources to Cloud Customer.
11. Cloud Customer runs jobs/tasks on allocated resources.
12. Cloud Customer gets the results.
13. Cloud Customer pays price to the Cloud Providers.
14. End

Table 4.2 Notation used in the chapter

Notation	Description
l	Number of VM types
n	Number of Cloud providers
a	Attribute vector
b^c	Required number of VMs by customer c
t^c	Total time for requested bundle
z	Number of QoS metrics
Q^c	QoS metrics values
b^i	Available VMs bundle at ith provider
Q^i	Set of QoS metrics of bundle ith
pp^i	Quoted price by ith provider for bundle b^i
ftp^i	Final trade price for ith provider

4.5 Truthful Combinatorial Reverse Auction in Cloud (TCRA)

From Sect. 4.3, one can observe that a sufficiently good number of models are available for single-unit single-item reverse auction that allocates resources using reverse auction. Some of these models are truthful as well. However, it has been noticed that in the combinatorial auction, allocation of resources has been given more focus in most of the reverse auction models. This encouraged us to formulate a Truthful Combinatorial Reverse Auction (TCRA) stressing on the truthfulness. This paves the way for the design of such type of auction that tackles other challenges in combinatorial reverse auction. It helps to understand the role of reverse auction for Cloud resource provisioning. Table 4.2 describes the notation used in this chapter.

4.5.1 Formulation of TCRA

User's Requirement

Let us assume that there are l types of VM and each VM is characterized by an attribute vector $(a_1, a_2, a_3, \ldots, a_l)$ where $a_1 < a_2 < a_3 < \cdots < a_l$. A customer c requires a set of l types of resources represented by b^c, i.e. $b^c = \left(q_1^c, q_2^c, q_3^c, \ldots, q_l^c\right)$. For example, q_1^c denotes the quantity of VMs of type 1 needed to c. c needs b^c for t^c time unit. Since in auction, provider may allocate spare resources to the customer, t^c will help the providers in the formation of bundle. c specifies z QoS metrics, i.e. $Q^c = \left(Q_1^c, Q_2^c \ldots, Q_z^c\right)$ as the set of value of QoS metrics that customer expects from winning providers. Customer submit its requirement, i.e. b^c and Q^c to the auctioneer to conduct an auction for the winner selection and the pricing.

Start of Auction by the Auctioneer

After receiving the requirement of customer, auctioneer prepares the call for proposal (CFP) specifying b^c, t^c and Q^c as given in Eq. (4.1) and publishes it in the market to start the auction.

$$\text{CFP} = \left(b^c, t^c, Q^c\right) \tag{4.1}$$

Submission of Bids by the Bidders

Let us assume that there are n providers, i.e. $(p_1, p_2, p_3, \ldots, p_n)$. Each provider p_i has available quantity of set of l types of VMs, i.e. $b^i = \left(q_1^i, q_2^i, q_3^i, \ldots, q_l^i\right)$ and pp^i is the price which p_i for b^i, i.e. quoted price. p_i also mentions QoS metrics $Q^i = \left(Q_1^i, Q_2^i \ldots, Q_z^i\right)$ for bundle b^i in the bid. Let Bid_p^i be the bid of the provider i which contains b^i, pp^i and Q^i as given in Eq. (4.2).

$$\text{Bid}_p^i = \left(b^i, pp^i, Q^i\right) \tag{4.2}$$

Auction Closing by Auctioneer

Since Cloud auctioneer cannot wait for indefinite period of time for the bids, a deadline T is introduced by the auctioneer after which auctioneer will not accept the bid. All the providers need to submit their bids as defined in Eq. (4.2) within the deadline T.

Winner Determination by Auctioneer

Cloud customer wants resources at minimum price with the desirable QoS; therefore, objective function in winner determination problem can be written as in Eq. (4.3) with capacity constraints represented using Eqs. (4.4) and (4.5).

$$\text{minimze} \sum_{i=1}^{n} s_i pp_i \tag{4.3}$$

subject to

$$\sum_{i=1}^{n} s_i q_j^i \geq q_j^c, j = 1, 2, \ldots, l \tag{4.4}$$

$$\sum_{i=1}^{n} s_i Q_j^i \geq Q_j^c, j = 1, 2, \ldots, z \tag{4.5}$$

$$s_i \in \{0, 1\}$$

where $s_i = 1$, if provider p_i wins and $s_i = 0$ otherwise.

Pricing Model

To make this auction model truthful, payment function is implemented using Clarke's mechanism [127]. Let us assume that $S = \{s_1, s_2, \ldots, s_n\}$ is the obtained solution of the winner determination problem and S^{-i} be the obtained solution when p_i is absent, i.e. $S^{-i} = \{s_1, s_2, \ldots, s_{i-1}, s_{i+1}, \ldots, s_n\}$. Final traded price, received by each provider p_i, can be written as in Eq. (4.6).

$$\text{ftp}^i = \text{pp}_i S_i + \sum_{j \neq i} \text{pp}_j S^{-i} - \sum \text{pp}_j S_j \qquad (4.6)$$

The payment received by each provider is the sum of the quoted cost of winner and the difference between the procurement cost without the winner and the procurement cost with the winner. Few theorems have been mentioned below to justify the properties of the TCRA model.

Theorem 1 *TCRA ensures individual rationality.*

Proof In TCRA, a combinatorial auction has been considered. Providers are single-minded bidders as discussed before. In this auction, if a provider wins, it gets payment using Clarke's mechanism. Therefore, the utility of winning providers is always positive and if providers do not win or do not participate, the utility becomes zero. This makes TCRA individual rational.

Theorem 2 *TCRA is incentive compatible; i.e., it is truthful.*

Proof In TCRA, the payment function is implemented using Clarke's mechanism [127]. Clarke's mechanism has already been established to be truthful, the proof for which is given in [127]. Therefore, TCRA proves to be incentive compatible.

Theorem 3 *TCRA is efficient.*

Proof Since the goal of TCRA is the minimization of cost, it always selects the providers with best bids, making it efficient.

Theorem 4 *TCRA is budget-balanced.*

Proof In TCRA, the price paid by the customer is equal to the payment received by the provider, resulting in a budget-balance.

4.5.2   Performance Evaluation of TCRA

Experimental study needs repeatable and controllable environment under different configurations and in Cloud creation of this type of environment for TCRA is not only tedious and costly but also time-consuming [34]. CloudAuction [158] is a simulator for Cloud auction implementation, but it supports combinatorial double auction without truthfulness and hence unsuitable for implementation of reverse auction in the Cloud. Therefore, TCRA has been simulated using MATLAB and instances of the problem are generated using uniform distribution. TCRA has been compared with C-DSIC [146] being one of the most cited contributions in reverse auction besides being truthful.

Three different scenarios are created for the analysis of TCRA. In Scenario 1, TCRA is compared with C-DSIC on the basis of the resource procurement cost. Execution time of C-DSIC is not compared with TCRA because TCRA is a combinatorial auction and a set of different type of resources is requested by the customer, while C-DSIC is single-unit single-item reverse auction. Therefore, the total time taken by C-DSIC depends on the execution time and deadline of each auction performed for each item in the requested set. In Scenario 2, procurement cost in TCRA is observed with the varying number of providers, while in Scenario 3, execution time of TCRA is observed with varying number of providers.

In both Scenario 2 and 3, for customer request generation Google cluster data is used [66]. There are three normalized values of CPU in Google cluster data, i.e. 0.25, 0.5 and 1.0. Therefore, three types of VM, i.e. $l = 3$ with capacity $C_1 = 0.25$, $C_2 = 0.5$, $C_3 = 1.0$ for each type of VM are considered for the experiment. In the current Cloud market, each provider has service limitation; e.g., Microsoft Azure has a default limitation of maximum 20 VMs for each user. Therefore, to simulate a real scenario, it is assumed that customer is aware of this limitation and a provider can provide only 20 maximum instances of a particular VM type.

Scenario 1: Comparison of TCRA and C-DSIC

TCRA is a combinatorial auction, while C-DSIC is a single-unit single-item auction. Formation of bundle in combinatorial auction requires the interest of customers in a particular bundle and their experience in additional understanding of auction's dynamics [153]. Bundling in combinatorial auction itself is a research challenge [65, 153]. Here, for simplicity, only discount is considered; i.e., provider gives some discount on the bundle which is a combination of several resources. The customer gets the better price for the bundle in comparison with the individual resources.

Three types of VMs have been considered for the experimental purposes. Their price is considered in such a way that the price of VM2 is greater than VM1 and the price of VM3 is greater than VM2. To generate the price of VMs for various providers, CLOUDORADO [48] is observed. CLOUDORADO is a Web service that provides comparison of various providers for various computing capacities on the basis of different criteria. Price of VM1, i.e. p_1, is randomly taken between [0.1, 0.2], price of VM2, i.e. p_2, is randomly taken between $[p_1 \times 1.5, p_1 \times 1.8]$, and p_3 is taken randomly $[p_2 \times 1.5, p_2 \times 1.8]$. This gives the importance to each VM with the logic that the low capacity VM should have a lower price. Other simulation parameters are presented in Table 4.3. Each experiment is performed 200 times and the average is taken to generate more precise results as shown in Fig. 4.2, which

Table 4.3 Simulation parameters

Parameters	Description
Types of VMs	3 (VM1, VM2, VM3)
Normalized value of CPU of VMs required by customer (float)	(0.25, 0.5, 1.0)
Range of normalized value of CPU of VMs (float)	VM1 [0.25, 0.5), VM2 [0.5, 1.0), VM3 [1.0, 1.5)
Quantity of VMs (integer)	VM1 [0, 20], VM2 [0, 20], VM3 [0, 20]
Requested quantity of VMs by customer (integer)	VM1 [100], VM2 [100], VM3 [100]
Number of providers (integer)	100
Value of QoS, reputation, fairness (float)	[1, 1, 1]

Fig. 4.2 Resource procurement cost as different discount rate

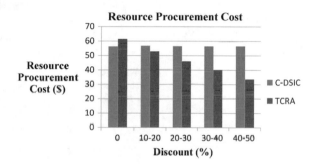

depicts the resource procurement cost on various discount rates for the two: C-DSIC and TCRA.

From Fig. 4.2, it can be observed that when there is no discount, C-DSIC performs better. But TCRA reports a better performance than C-DSIC even when the discount is low, i.e. 10–20%. Accordingly, as the discount increases, resource procurement cost decreases in TCRA, while it remains same in C-DSIC.

Scenario 2: Effect of the Number of Providers on the Procurement Cost

In Google trace, TraceVersion1 is created from one cluster over the duration of 7 h. To hide the details of machines, normalized value of CPU is provided with each task. We extracted three relevant fields for each task: Task ID (identity of task), Time and Normalized CPU value. To create on auction round, tasks in 300 s are grouped, and thus, total 76 auction rounds are created. In each auction round, to identify the workload, the method given in [168] is considered. This workload helps to identify all three types of number of VMs. Let us assume that λ is the workload for which customer needs VMs. Sum of normalized value of CPU for each task in 300 s is considered as workload for that auction round. Method to identify the number of VMs of each type is given in Eqs. (4.7) and (4.8).

Table 4.4 Simulation parameters

Parameters	Description
Types of VMs	3 (VM1, VM2, VM3)
Normalized value of CPU of VMs required by customer (float)	(0.25, 0.5, 1.0)
Range of Normalized value of CPU of VMs (float)	VM1 [0.25, 0.5), VM2 [0.5, 1.0), VM3 [1.0, 1.5)
Quantity of VMs (integer)	VM1 [0, 20], VM2 [0, 20], VM3 [0, 20]
Range of price (float)	$[1–10]
Number of providers (integer)	50–500
Value of QoS, reputation, fairness (float)	[1, 1, 1]

Fig. 4.3 Resource procurement cost in TCRA with increasing number of providers

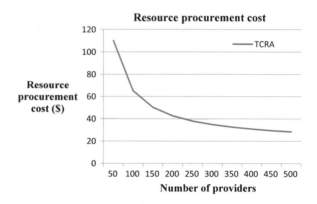

$$\text{minimize} \sum_{j=1}^{l} q_j p_j \tag{4.7}$$

$$\text{subject to} \sum_{j=1}^{l} q_j C_j \geq \lambda \tag{4.8}$$

where q_j is the quantity of VM of type j to handle the workload λ. This is an optimization problem and can be solved using integer linear programming.

Simulation parameters, for this scenario, have been listed in Table 4.4. For each auction of 76 rounds, experiments were performed 200 times and the average is taken for more precise result. Since there are 76 auction rounds, it is difficult to show all the results. Therefore, the average of the results of 76 rounds is taken and presented in Fig. 4.3.

From Fig. 4.3, it can be observed that as the number of providers increases the resource procurement cost decreases. It can be concluded from the experiments that a tough competition among the providers ultimately benefits the customer.

Fig. 4.4 Execution time of
TCRA with increasing
number of providers

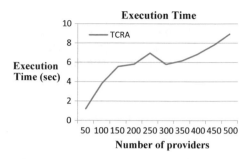

Scenario 3: Effect of the Number of Providers on the Execution Time

In this scenario, the effect of the number of providers on the execution time of
TCRA is observed. The simulation parameters are same as shown in Table 4.3, and
the average of the obtained results from 76 auction rounds is presented in Fig. 4.4.

From Fig. 4.4, it can be observed that the execution time reported by TCRA
increases with the increase in the number of the providers. Execution time of TCRA
thus becomes higher for a large number of providers because of its implementation
using linear programming which becomes complex with the increasing number of
input parameters.

4.5.3 Discussion on TCRA

The proposed TCRA ensures truthfulness by giving the incentive to the providers for
revealing their true value of the offered bundle of resources. The proposed TCRA is
designed to be both combinatorial and truthful, but its execution time is high. TCRA
is presented here to give a better understanding of the combinatorial reverse auction,
encouraging the researchers to design and solve the combinatorial reverse auction
using some heuristics in such a way that the allocation of the resource and pricing
are done in polynomial time while meeting maximum auction properties.

TCRA has been compared with a baseline model C-DSIC, and it is observed
that TCRA performs better when a bundle of resources is required by the user. The
decrease in the resource procurement cost on the increase of number of providers
proves that a healthy competition among providers is beneficial for the customers.
However, in TCRA, execution time is reportedly higher when the number of providers
participating in the auction is high. Further, in TCRA it has been assumed that
the customer defines a time period for which it needs the requested resources. A
possibility may arise that the customer needs to wait for some time to get access to
these resources. But once the customer gets the resource, there is no interruption.
Applications of this type of auction can be multi-tier Web applications, workflow
applications, multi-threaded applications, map-reduce applications, etc. If the time
period is not specified by the customer or the time period is controlled by the provider,

the resources can be abruptly terminated as in the case of spot instances being out-of-bid situation. In such type of auction, either applications should have a flexible start and stop time such as data analysis, background processing or fault-tolerant mechanism is need to be implemented [12].

4.6   Issues and Challenges

Reverse auction has the potential and possesses a good possibility of its implementation in real Cloud in future. This section lists and elaborates some important issues and challenges that are possible during and after the implementation of reverse auction in Cloud resource provisioning.

Unambiguous Design

Unclear specification of the customer's requirements and designing of ambiguous auction rules may create an unresponsive market. In such situation, a provider may leave the market which destroys the relationship between the customer and providers. In the absence of an actual implemented work, an unambiguous design of reverse auction considering all the necessary Cloud aspect is an open challenge.

Switching Cost

The degree of switching cost is also an important factor using auction [23]. Customer has to bear the inevitable switching cost, when it chooses a new provider. High switching cost can affect the customer badly in the long run. Though, it is more related to the interoperability issue, it still demands a good consideration by the auction designer in the winner determination.

Maintaining the Competition

A provider, quoting low, may prevent the winning chances of a higher-quoting price provider who eventually may get frustrated and may even leave the auction. In the absence of high-quoting price bidders, low-quoting bidders can control the market as well as decision-making in the price. This may increase the price of the resources with the market being in their full control. This scenario is referred as the bidder drop problem [91]. A strong competition, among the providers, is essential for the reduction of the procurement cost which requires sufficient number of providers in the market. The literature suggests that in auction, participation of some k bidders is always equal or more beneficial compared to the participation of k-1 bidders [121]. To prevent the oligopoly of powerful providers and to maintain a sufficient number of providers, some mechanisms need to be designed and implemented that provide fairness in the Cloud market and give positive feelings about the reverse auction to the providers. There are many ways to consider fairness in auction, e.g. priority and reservation price [122]. Profit sharing is also a method to provide fairness [200, 202]. For short-term benefit, implementation of fairness may not seem well, but it has been proven that for the long-term benefits of the participants, it performs fairly well [91, 123].

SLA Management

Providers may get involved in collusion. To win the auction, a provider may offer resources at a very low price during bidding. But after winning the auction, it may try to wriggle out its promise when the promised qualities of resources in the bid are not favourable to the provider. It is also possible that the winning provider may deliver different QoS than promised during bidding. To handle this challenge, a penalty can be imposed on those providers that give false QoS assurance in order to win the auction. Auctioneer can act as a mediator, in this situation, and deduct some money from the payment on the basis of the actual delivered QoS. This helps in maintaining the utility of the customer and simultaneously discouraging the providers from false bidding.

Consideration of Non-price Attributes in the Winner Determination

Other than price, QoS is an important parameter in the provider selection that cannot be ignored [1]. Other non-price attributes such as reputation of the provider cannot be ignored. Accounting of price only in winner determination is not justified. Reverse auction in Cloud is designed in such a way that both price and non-price attributes are used in the determination of winners. Most of the works, which considered non-price attributes in reverse auction in Cloud computing, did not use them to prioritize the bidders.

Computational Complexity of the Combinatorial Auction

Currently, availability of VMs for specific purposes (e.g. Amazon provides R3 instances for memory intensive applications) provides ability to the customer to express request in terms of the set of resources which are dependent and complimentary. In the discussed scenario, combinatorial auction is the most suitable and extended form of auction for Cloud services where a set of resources is available for the auction in the form of a bundle [50]. As such, combinatorial auction is a NP-hard problem [50].

Truth Revelation

In order to solve the cost minimization problem, the auctioneer should know the true value of the resources. But providers are often reluctant to reveal the true value as they are autonomous, rational and intelligent [127]. Autonomy here signifies that the providers and users are not bound to comply with the action of the central authority, i.e. auctioneer or other participants. Rational means participants are self-interested agents; i.e., they participate in the auction in order to maximize their own objectives, and intelligent means participants are able to perform computation to decide their strategy on the basis of their own knowledge or expected behaviour of other participants. In other words, in the competitive and commercial Cloud market, increasing number of Cloud providers are focused towards increasing their revenue in comparison with the utility of the users; i.e., the providers may act selfishly with private information about their resources. Therefore, in reverse auction, a user should not only trust the information provided by the providers but should act carefully as there is always a possibility of misrepresentation of information by the providers.

Bundling

Combinatorial auction generates significant revenue and maximizes market economic efficiency by allocating the resources to those who value them the most [116]. Bundling in combinatorial auction is also an important issue. Bundle formation requires decisions on the bundle size, types of VMs placed in the bundle, number of each type of VMs, non-price attributes of the bundle, price of bundle, to name a few [153]. These decisions require the understanding of the auction's dynamics and interest of customers in bundles [187]. Market history can really be helpful in this regard. But generally the market does not reveal the information of bundles with the pricing done by the providers only. It only reveals the information of the winning bundle and the traded price. A bidder's decision-making would depend on its winning/losing bundle, its risk and its attitude towards the market [130].

Few Other Issues

More number of bidders make the winner selection problem more complex. This requires some techniques that qualify only the most suitable bidders in the auction. Configurable offer in multi-attribute reverse auction is also a challenge. Generally, it is assumed that the offered quantity, its price and non-price attributes are fixed. But a negotiation over price and non-price attributes in multi-attribute reverse auction may make Cloud market even more efficient through an effective information exchange about the preferences of the providers and the customers. In the case of auction, reliability is an important issue. Therefore, fault tolerance schemes like checkpointing and work migration must be implemented as done in the case of spot instances. Providers may participate in the auction not only to win but to understand the market. Customer may perform reverse auction repeatedly to force the incumbent providers to reduce their prices. Customer also may bid low as a phantom provider or may include unviable and unqualified providers to stimulate the competition. Designing of auction mechanism to prevent such type of activities is also a challenge.

4.7   Summary

Allocation of resources, using reverse auction, is an active area of research. This chapter details the description of reverse auction and describes its benefits to understand the basics of reverse auction. The applicability of reverse auction in Cloud has been explained with its attributes. Various auction properties, a reverse auction should ensure, are discussed. An investigation of existing works in the reverse auction is presented to provide an overview of the state of the art in reverse auction in Cloud computing. The existing works are also evaluated on the basis of auction properties to help researchers to understand their strengths and weaknesses. A market view for

reverse auction is discussed to understand the basic steps in designing the real implementation of the reverse auction. The work further proposes a truthful combinatorial
auction model TCRA and its comparison with a baseline model leading the way on
how to design an auction with the desired goals. Open research issues have been identified listing several research opportunities for the research community in the Cloud
computing. This work intends to encourage the researchers to design reverse auction
mechanism in Cloud resource allocation by resolving various discussed issues. It
also appeals the Cloud industry to come forward and support the reverse auction that
benefits both the service providers and the consumers.

Chapter 5
Double Auction-Based Cloud Resource Provisioning

Abstract In double auction, both the user and the provider bid in the market. In this chapter, a detailed description of double auction mechanisms and their applicability in Cloud market is discussed. Various auction properties, that a double auction mechanism should satisfy, have also been discussed and deliberated. A detailed survey of related work in double auction-based Cloud resource provisioning and pricing is provided. A truthful multi-unit double auction-based model is also presented to help and motivate the Cloud researchers/academicians to design such efficient and truthful mechanisms for the Cloud market. Finally, research challenges and issues are identified with future research possibilities.

5.1 Introduction

In Cloud computing market, a good number of Cloud providers offer their services to be used by the Cloud users to perform their tasks. It creates a good competition at both sides in the Cloud market; i.e., users compete with each other to obtain the limited amount of resources and providers compete with each other to offer their services in order to increase their revenue. This type of market environment can be modelled using double auction in which biding happens from both sides of the market. This type of auction can be used to design unbiased optimal market strategy in the Cloud market.

As available in the literature, few resource allocation models based on double auction have been proposed in the past. For these models, the allocation algorithms have been designed using supply and demand principle. First, bids of the users and providers both are analysed and thereafter demanded and available quantities of the resources are matched to obtain an equilibrium price. However, the mechanisms proposed so far give less attention to pricing and emphasize more on resource allocation in the whole double auction mechanism. Basic properties, to be satisfied by an auction mechanism, are missing in the mechanism designed for the Cloud market due to market complexity, heterogeneous resource configurations, variable demand and supply. There are some impossibility results also regarding the satisfiability of

© The Author(s) 2018
G. Baranwal et al., *Auction Based Resource Provisioning in Cloud Computing*,
SpringerBriefs in Computer Science, https://doi.org/10.1007/978-981-10-8737-0_5

all these properties by a double auction mechanism in the literature of economics. Considering the trade-off among these properties, researchers designed the mechanisms which satisfy a subset of properties. Incentive compatibility or truthfulness has been the main requirement for the mechanism designers due to its importance and a necessity for a viable and efficient market.

Although various double auction mechanisms have been proposed for the Cloud market, till now these mechanisms have not been implemented in a real Cloud market. There are some double auction mechanisms which have been implemented in laboratory e-market, but auction properties are not guaranteed [196]. In future, it is inevitable to have a number of organizations/companies with varying Cloud services. A stiff competition is expected in the Cloud market due to the presence of these users and providers. Various properties of double auction such as efficient resource allocation, least time, dynamic pricing, consideration of supply and demand principle make it suitable for modelling the both sides' competition in the Cloud market. This chapter presents a study on basic double auction mechanisms with their properties and their applicability in the context of Cloud computing from a mechanism design point of view.

The rest of the chapter is as follows. A detailed study on basic double auction mechanisms with their properties, their applicability in Cloud computing and the literature survey has been given in Sects. 5.2 and 5.3. In Sect. 5.4, a Truthful multi-unit Double Auction for Cloud Computing (TDACC) model is presented along with their auction properties. An illustrative example is given in Sect. 5.5 to understand the mechanism in a clear manner. Various issues and challenges, for the double auction-based Cloud computing market, have been discussed in Sect. 5.6. Section 5.7 summarizes the chapter.

5.2 Double Auction

There are various competitive markets such as bonds, stocks and commodities, Internet market in which double auction can be used for trading or exchange of goods or resources [29]. Double auction is based on the demand and supply principle. In general, after submission of bids from both the sides, the auctioneer sets a final trade price on which supply equals the demand. This price is called the equilibrium price.

Double auction mechanism, in a competitive market, prevents the monopoly and handles both sides' competition well. Double auction is more computationally and economically efficient than single-sided auction when market participants are very large in number [36, 138, 144]. Single-sided auctions, e.g. procurement auctions, are suitable only when there are less number of Cloud users. In case of large number of users, computational burden increases on the provider side due to repeated bidding behaviour. This whole process is also tedious as all the possible auction outcomes are contemplated by the provider. This reduces the possible trades or transactions, especially in combinatorial auctions [199]. In addition, in the long run, an efficiency maximizing double action mechanism yields more revenue than several repeated single one-sided auctions [197].

5.2.1   Double Auction Properties

There are certain properties that should be fulfilled by a double auction mechanism similar to other types of auctions (reverse and forward auction) as discussed in previous chapters.

Economic Efficiency

A double auction is economically efficient if it maximizes the total social welfare or surplus (sum of valuations of all participants) of the market. This can be achieved by trading the resources among most eligible users (with highest valuations) and providers (with lowest offer prices).

Individual Rationality

This property ensures that a participant utility is always nonnegative, i.e. $U_i^u, U_j^p \geq 0\ \forall i, j$ where U_i^u and U_j^p are the utilities of ith user and jth provider, respectively.

Budget-Balance

If a mechanism is budget-balanced, then the sum of the payments of users is equal to or greater than the total money received by all the providers. Budget-balance is a strong requirement in double auction mechanism. Conceptually, this property ensures the viability and sustainability of the market by ensuring that the market maker/designer/auctioneer is not at loss in conducting the auction.

Computational Efficiency

This property ensures that the mechanism is computationally tractable and implementable in polynomial time.

Incentive Compatibility or Truthfulness

A double auction mechanism is incentive compatible/truthful if revealing true information is dominant strategy for each participant; i.e., a participant's utility will be maximum if it bids truthfully. Vickrey auction is an example of truthful auction mechanism [186].

There are some impossibility results regarding satisfiability of all the properties by a double auction mechanism [125]. Therefore, researchers have focused on the trade-off and proposed various mechanisms that satisfy a subset of these properties. In double auction scenario, budget-balance and truthfulness are the strong requirements and both of these ensure the sustainability and viability of the auction. In case of efficiency, computational efficiency and economic efficiency conflict with each other in some environment such as combinatorial bidding.

5.2.2 Applicability of Double Auction in Cloud Computing

The size of the Cloud market has been increased tremendously in recent years due to the popularity of Cloud computing. Currently, a number of Cloud providers offer Cloud services to their users with different pricing and varying QoS. Cloud offers significant cost saving for the start-ups and businesses. This has resulted and will increase with tremendous increase in the number of Cloud users. In future, more and more users and start-ups are expected to adopt the Cloud platform. These Cloud users want to execute their tasks on Cloud resources with minimal price and better QoS. A Cloud provider wants to maximize its profit or revenue by maximizing the resource utilization and providing the Cloud services at an optimal price with desirable QoS. Therefore, both the users and providers have their objectives and compete in the market strategically. As discussed earlier, double auction is one of the many ways to model competition at both sides in auction-based market.

Although, in the literature, models based on all types of auction have been reported, on of date only forward auction-based mechanisms have been implemented by Amazon for selling their unutilized spot instances [12]. Therefore, double auction-based Cloud market is a futuristic scenario and its actual implementation depends upon addressing its various assumptions like interoperability, request indivisibility. However, the possibility of double auction-based Cloud market is potentially good. In this section, the applicability of double auction-based mechanisms in Cloud market is explored in detail.

With the tremendous increment in the number of Cloud users, multiple Cloud providers also started offering the Cloud services to fulfil the demand. Availability of multiple providers resulted in the multi-Cloud [140], inter-Cloud [183] and Cloud federation [87]. In multi-Cloud, there are multiple providers in the market and user can select the best one or even take the services from more than one provider. In federated Cloud, multiple service providers cooperate with each other to fulfil the users' requests. Inter-Cloud is used to cover all scenario of availability of multiple Cloud providers in the market. Bernstein et al. [25] define inter-Cloud as "Cloud of Clouds"; i.e., inter-Cloud is a unified mesh of Clouds based on open standards to provide interoperability. Inter-Cloud has various benefits such as better QoS deliverance to users, less energy consumption, better services even at peak times, cost efficiency for both the user and the provider. Therefore, researchers and Cloud professionals are focusing on the implementation of the inter-Cloud [68]. Recently, a report on Cloud market by [137] studies the Cloud market in different countries. The report finds that most of the Cloud providers are based in USA, while Japan is the topmost market for Cloud services export. That way, providers from the European countries are striving to attract the users and inter-Cloud is a possible solution for the better services. For this, European Union has funded a good number of inter-Cloud projects, e.g. MODAClouds [119], Cloud4SOA [46], TClouds [180], REMICS [152]. All the inter-Cloud-related projects that are either completed or in progress are listed in [68]. There are some organizations such as Cloud Computing Interoperability Forum (CCIF), Open Cloud Manifesto, DMTF Cloud Standards Incubator that are trying to design some open standard between the service providers. For example, Open Virtualization Format (OVF) is one of the standards supported by some providers, which allows the users to switch from one provider to another [183].

5.3 Related Work on Double Auction in Cloud

Some related works, which apply double auction mechanism for the Cloud resources, are as follows.

Double auctions were used in grid computing environment before Cloud computing for provisioning and sharing of resources [79, 95, 179]. Combinatorial double auction-based resource allocation schemes for grid market are proposed in [95] in which grid users have combinatorial bidding structure. The work claims, through the experimental studies, that the proposed mechanism satisfies the incentive compatibility property. However, no theoretical or analytical proof is given for the above claim. [76] extends three double auction mechanisms, i.e. Preston-McAfee double auction (PMDA), threshold price double auction (TPDA) and continuous double auction (CDA) for resource allocation in grid. The authors show that CDA outperforms among all the three mechanisms in terms of resource utilization. Motivated by the work done in [57], [76] proposed a resource allocation model based on continuous double auction for the grid market. In the model, user's bid value increases with the decrease in the average mean remaining time or the number of remaining resources. The reason, for the above bidding behaviour, is that a user will try to finish its running tasks as soon as possible by acquiring more resources by bidding with higher values. Provider's bid lies between its offer price and maximum price and is determined by the total workload. The findings claim that the model performs better in terms of mean trade price, fairness deviation and resource utilization.

To find the winning consumer and provider, besides calculating the trading prices in the Cloud market, double auction is applied in [191]. Cell membrane optimization (CMO) is used for resource allocation in the Cloud resource management framework. The bid value of cloud resource consumer (CRC) increases if it fails to get its required resources, while the bid value of cloud resource provider (CRP) decreases if it fails in selling its resources. Trading prices were calculated by taking the average of both the bid values of user and provider. After finding the winners, resources are allocated using CMO technique. The proposed model is simulated in CloudSim. However, auction properties were not discussed in the work.

A uniform, competitive and flexible framework is proposed in [167] for buying and selling of Cloud resources in the Cloud market. In addition, an optimal pricing strategy and a Bayesian game among users and providers were also proposed for the same. However, the proposed model lacks in an appropriate simulation study. An economically efficient marketplace for Cloud computing using double auction mechanisms is proposed in [62] by considering two types of markets—forward market and spot market. Mixed-integer programming (MIP) technique was used for the service allocation. However, the model is not incentive compatible and does not work well when market size increases. A Cloud market model based on continuous double auction is also proposed in [57] for Cloud service allocation. A computational Cloud simulator JADE (Java Agent Development Framework) is used for the simulation.

A combinatorial double auction-based resource allocation and pricing model (CDARA) for Cloud is proposed in [158]. The authors considered the combinatorial bidding structure for both the user and the provider. They extended the works of [95, 209] and proposed a greedy-based resource allocation algorithm. For calculating the final trade prices, average of bid prices of the matching Cloud customers and providers is considered. However, CDARA is not incentive compatible. A double multi-attribute auction (DMAA)-based resource allocation model is proposed in [194]. For resource allocation and pricing, mean variance optimization (MVO) method and support vector machine (SVM) were used. However, the model did not describe the auction properties such as economic efficiency and incentive compatibility.

Most of the double auction mechanisms, designed for the Cloud market, have focused on maximizing the total valuation, maximizing the revenue or minimizing the total user cost in the market [89, 158]. A few works considered the egalitarian-based approach by implementing the fairness in the resource allocation process. A fair multi-attribute combinatorial double auction model (FMCDAM) for resource allocation in Cloud computing is proposed in [18]. The work considered two previous works [142, 158] in their model and proposed an efficient and fair double auction mechanism using greedy allocation and average pricing method. Several attributes, other than price, e.g. QoS, reputation, fairness, were considered in the FMCDAM. The work imposed a penalty on the providers and their reputation decreases if they do not provide the resources with quoted QoS; i.e., offered QoS levels are not met as promised. The decrease in the reputation further lowers the chance of winning the auction in successive rounds. The work also implemented fairness in the mechanism, thus reducing the bidder drop problem. Almost all the auction properties are discussed in the work from a mechanism design point of view. FMCDAM satisfied nearly all properties except incentive compatibility.

Sun et al. [177] took a different approach to tackle the malicious behaviour of Cloud users and providers using the feedback rating-based reputation system and proposed a combinatorial double auction for resource allocation in Cloud. In this work, group search optimization techniques were used for the winner determination problem (WDP) in the allocation phase and back-propagation neural network was used for the pricing of the traded resources. Similar to the work of [177], [193] proposed a Paddy Field Algorithm (PFA) for resource allocation. However, auction properties were not described in both the works.

Two novel incentive-compatible mechanisms, namely continuous double auction (CDA) mechanism and modified Vickrey (MVA) mechanism, are proposed in [198]. They focused on the automatic and scalable resource allocation in the self-organizing Cloud. For providers, incentive-compatible mechanisms were designed which offer incentives to the providers to reveal their valuations truthfully. Cloud users select appropriate Cloud resources with minimum cost and desired quality based on the proposed CDA mechanism which considers competition at both side. However, the mechanism is not individual rational and not truthful for the Cloud consumers. Further, QoS was not considered for resource allocation and pricing.

In [143] as well, CDA mechanisms for dynamic pricing of the resources in heterogeneous Cloud market have been proposed. Exponential smoothing function is used by the Cloud user for the resource valuation, and bids were generated using zero-intelligence strategy. The work was simulated in GridSim simulator with the auction framework. A family of combinatorial double auction mechanisms for Cloud systems based on greedy method is proposed in [41]. The work focused mainly on designing the resource allocation algorithms and proposed two separate algorithms for homogeneous and heterogeneous resource configurations. These algorithms were analysed in terms of allocative efficiency, resource utilization and social welfare. However, the work did not propose any payment mechanism in combinatorial double auction-based model.

An IR, IC, ex-post BB and approximately efficient multi-unit double auction for inter-Cloud VM trading among users and providers in federated Cloud environment is proposed in [94]. The model focuses on maximizing the social welfare and profit of the providers by implementing a dynamic job scheduling algorithm. Zheng et al. [214] proposed ex-post BB and grouping-based truthful double auction mechanisms for multi-Cloud environments in which providers offer the network services to the Cloud tenants. In a similar work, Lee et al. [89] proposed a real-time double auction-based Cloud market framework in which Cloud users have combinatorial bidding structure. The work also proposed a group formation mechanism in which both users and providers formed a group based on their demand and supply. The allocation algorithm, proposed in the work, optimally allocates the Cloud instances to the users. The mechanism details all the auction properties and satisfies almost all of these properties, except incentive compatibility. K-double auction rule [59] is used for trade price calculation in the work.

In a similar work, in [178], VM allocation mechanisms based on combinatorial double auction are proposed. It incorporates the group buying behaviour of users for availing the VMs at discounted prices. Quantity-based discount was adopted in the model, and two mechanisms were proposed based on the greedy allocation and critical proportional value pricing method. Further, these mechanisms were compared with [158] in terms of total social welfare, resource utilization and total winning users. However, truthfulness was proved only for the users' side. A combinatorial double auction-based resource allocation, maximizing the social welfare, was also proposed in [156]. In the work, WDP problem is solved using imperialist competitive algorithm, whereas Kth-pricing was used for payment settlement among the users and the providers.

5.3.1 Comparative Study Based on Auction Properties

The above works reveal that designing truthful double auction mechanisms in complex environment such as discriminatory pricing, combinatorial and multidimen-

Table 5.1 A comparison of double auction models

Double auction in Cloud (reference)	Auction properties			
	EE	IC	IR	BB
[167]	✓	✗	✓	✓
[158]	✓	✗	✗	✓
[62]	✓	✗	✓	✓
[95]	✓	✗	✗	✓
[53]	✓	✗	✓	–
[94]	✗	✓	✓	✓
[214]	✗	✓	✓	✓
[89]	✓	✗	✓	✓
[44]	✗	✗	✗	✓
[178]	✗	✓ (user only)	✓	✓
[198]	✓	✓ (provider only)	✗	✓
[191]	✓	✗	✗	✗
[18]	✓	✗	✗	✓
[156]	✗	✗	✓	✓
[148]	✓	✗	✓	–
[203]	✗	✗	✓	✓
[57]	✓	✗	✓	–

EE economic efficiency, *IC* incentive compatible, *IR* individual rationality, *BB* budget-balance

sional bids, heterogeneous resource configurations is practically and theoretically difficult. Most of the mechanisms designed are truthful for one side of market participants, i.e. either for the user or for the provider. A comparative study of all above-discussed works in terms of auction properties is given in Table 5.1.

5.4   Truthful Multi-unit Double Auction for Cloud Computing

The comparative study on double auction mechanisms in Cloud reveals that most of the works such as [43, 53, 89, 191] focus on the resource allocation problem while giving little attention to resource pricing, mainly truthful pricing schemes for both user and provider. The model, proposed in this work, has been designed and discussed from a mechanism design (MD) point of view with a description of all MD properties theoretically as well as practically. The proposed model can be used by the researchers and professionals as a basic framework (baseline) for designing double auction mechanisms which are truthful for both the user and the provider.

A Cloud market is like any other auction-based market where some allocation and pricing mechanism are applied keeping in mind some technical details such as VM resource configurations and other Cloud system details. A Cloud provider generally provides the resources in the form of virtual machines (VMs) which consist of different resources, e.g. CPU, memory, storage, network. For example, Amazon offers various types of VMs (EC2 Instances) using dynamic pricing schemes such as spot pricing. In this, a user can bid for a single VM at one time. If one requires more VMs, one has to bid repeatedly. Recently, Amazon has started offering multiple similar type VMs using spot pools and spot fleets [12].

In this work, it is assumed that all the Cloud providers possess rack of servers in their respective data centres and homogeneous types of VMs can be provisioned on the users' requests. Here, VMs are traded in the proposed auction market. As main focus is on designing a truthful pricing schemes in double auction-based Cloud market, a simple Cloud environment is assumed in this work in which multiple Cloud users and providers are involved in buying and selling the resources and homogeneous types of VMs are available in the market. Multi-unit-demand by users and multi-unit supply by providers are considered in the work. More complex bidding structure such as combinatorial bidding can be considered but is difficult to design. The homogeneity of the VMs, considered in this work, is justified by the fact that recently some business professionals have proposed a common unit to measure virtual resources (CPU, memory, storage, etc.) offered by various providers [47]. For example, Amazon [145] defined "EC2 Compute Units" or ECUs as a measure of virtual computing power defined as a 40 ECU where one ECU is a standard unit (e.g. VM in this case) for computing. In the same manner, standard resource units can be proposed for other resources such as storage, bandwidth. A market maker/auctioneer/broker is responsible for defining common measuring units for all types of resources provided by the various providers.

The auction model, considered in this work, is sealed-bid; i.e., the information of a participant's bid is private and known to herself only. All Cloud users and providers are rational, strategic and intelligent. They want to optimize their utility. For that, they can manipulate the market by false bidding which causes unfeasible trades in the market. Therefore, truthfulness is enforced into the auction mechanism for a sustainable and efficient market. For truthfulness, dominant strategy incentive-compatible mechanism is designed which ensures that a participant's utility will be maximum if the participant reveals her information truthfully. Although the proposed work assumes simple Cloud environment, it gives a direction to design truthful double auction mechanisms for Cloud environment.

0. Begin
1. Auctioneer starts auction.
2. Users and Providers submit bids to auctioneer.
3. Auctioneer acknowledges the Users and Providers about their bids.
4. Auctioneer closes the auction.

5. Auctioneer informs the Users and Providers about closing of the auction.
6. Auctioneer evaluates the bids of Users and Providers and finds allocation results (the winning set of users and providers).
7. Auctioneer informs all the bidders about the allocation results.
8. Winning Providers allocate the resources to winning Cloud Users based on the allocation result.
9. Auctioneer calculates the payments to be made by the users to the providers based on the allocated quantity.
10. Auctioneer informs the trade prices to the Cloud Users and the Providers.
11. Cloud Users pay to the Cloud Providers according to the final trade prices.
12. End

After submitting the bids, auctioneer closes the auction. Winning set of users and providers is found using the proposed allocation mechanism. Auctioneer communicates the results to the user and the provider. After allocation, final trade prices are calculated that users pay to the provider for utilizing the resources. The steps used in the model are given below in the box.

The notation, used in the model, is given in Table 5.2.

As discussed, the main focus is on designing double auction mechanisms that satisfy the truthfulness property. There are multiple stages in the proposed double auction. First, reserve prices are calculated for both the user and the provider by finding the non-winning users and providers in unit-demand and unit-supply demand case. A user's reserve price will always be higher than the provider's reserve price. After that, it finds the total allocated quantity using these reserved prices. Truthful payments are then calculated for both users and providers using VCG pricing rule [45, 67, 186].

Let N be the number of users and providers, and $\mathcal{N}^U$ & $\mathcal{N}^P$ be the set of users and providers, respectively. Users and providers are indexed using $i \in \mathcal{N}^U = \{1, 2, \ldots, N\}$ and $j \in \mathcal{N}^P = \{1, 2, \ldots, N\}$, respectively. Let K-unit of VMs are to be traded in the market. Let b^i be the valuation vector of ith user and $b^i = (b^i_1, b^i_2, \ldots, b^i_K)$, where b^i_k be the user ith marginal valuation for the kth unit of VM. Let p^j be the price vector of jth provider and $p^j = (p^j_1, p^j_2, \ldots, p^j_K)$ where p^j_k is the marginal ask price of offering kth unit of VMs. Diminishing marginal valuations for users and increasing marginal prices for providers are considered in the work, i.e. $b^i_k \geq b^i_{k+1}$ and $p^j_k \leq p^j_{K+1}$ $\forall i \in \mathcal{N}^U, j \in \mathcal{N}^P, k \in \{1, 2, \ldots, K\}$.

Reserve Price Calculation

The reserve prices for the user and the provider are calculated using the marginal valuation and cost/ask price of first unit of VMs. For this, a unit-demand and supply case (unit-VM case) is considered in which a user's request is restricted to single-unit-VM case and each provider offers a single unit of VMs. Let b_{first} and p_{first} be the users' marginal valuation vector and providers' marginal valuation for the first unit of VMs in sorted order, i.e. $b_{\text{first}} = (b^{\text{first}}_1, b^{\text{first}}_2, \ldots, b^{\text{first}}_N)$ and $p_{\text{first}} = (p^{\text{first}}_1, p^{\text{first}}_2, \ldots, p^{\text{first}}_N)$

Table 5.2 Notation used

Notation	Description	Notation	Description
N	Total number of Cloud users and providers	$\mathcal{N}^U$	Set of Cloud users
K	Number of VMs	$\mathcal{N}^P$	Set of Cloud providers
b_k^i	Marginal valuation of ith user's for the kth unit of VM	p_k^j	Marginal cost of jth provider for kth unit of VM
U_j^p	Utility of jth provider	U_i^u	Utility of ith user
b^i	Marginal valuation vector of ith user	p^j	Marginal cost/ask price vector of jth provider
b_{first}	Users' marginal valuations for first unit of VMs	p_{first}	Providers' marginal costs for first unit of VMs
Q_{unit}	Number of VMs allocated in unit-item case	$\text{user}_1^{\text{win}}$	Set of winning users in unit-item case
$\text{user}_1^{\text{lose}}$	Set of losing users in unit-item case	$\text{prov}_1^{\text{win}}$	Set of winning providers in unit-item case
$\text{prov}_1^{\text{lose}}$	Set of losing providers in unit-item case	$U_{\text{weak}}^{\text{win}}$	User with the lowest marginal valuation for first unit among winning users
$U_{\text{strng}}^{\text{lose}}$	User with the highest marginal valuation for first unit among the losing users	$P_{\text{weak}}^{\text{win}}$	Provider with the highest marginal cost for first unit among winning providers
$P_{\text{strng}}^{\text{lose}}$	Provider with the highest marginal cost among the losing providers	$\text{price}_{\text{range}}^{\text{loser}}$	Loser-agent price range
$\text{Reserve}_{\text{user}}^{\text{price}}$	Reserve price for users	$\text{Reserve}_{\text{prov}}^{\text{price}}$	Reserve price for providers
$\text{Request}^{\text{total}}$	Total requested quantity	$\text{offer}^{\text{total}}$	Total offered quantity
Q^{traded}	Total allocated quantity	b	A permutation of users' valuation vectors
Q^{user}	Total number of VMs allocated to user	$b_{Q^{\text{traded}}}$	Marginal valuation vector of winning users of all the allocated units
Q_{user}^i	Number of VMs allocated to ith user	b_{user}^{-i}	Q^{user}-dimensional vector of marginal valuations of users except user i
b^{-i}	Marginal valuation vectors of all users except user i	Q^{prov}	Total number of VMs offered by all providers

(continued)

Table 5.2 (continued)

Notation	Description	Notation	Description
p	Permutation of providers' costs vectors	$p_{Q^{\text{traded}}}$	Marginal costs/ask prices vector of winning providers of all the allocated units
Q^j_{prov}	Number of VMs offered by jth provider	p^{-j}_{prov}	Q^{prov}-dimensional vector of marginal costs of providers except provider j
$\text{Reserve}^{\text{price}}_{\text{primary}}$	Primary reserve price	$\text{pay}^{\text{user}}_i$	Payment of ith user
$\text{pay}^{\text{prov}}_j$	Payment of jth provider	$\text{price}^{\text{win}}_{\text{range}}$	Winner-agent price range

where $b^{\text{first}}_q \geq b^{\text{first}}_{q+1}$ and $p^{\text{first}}_q \leq p^{\text{first}}_{q+1}$. A feasible trade quantity in unit-VM case can be found as $Q_{\text{unit}} = \max\{Q \in \{0, 1, 2, \ldots, N\} : b^{\text{first}}_Q > p^{\text{first}}_Q\}$. Using this, set of users and providers are identified which are able to trade in unit-VM case. Let user^{win}_1 be the set of users who successfully get a unit-VM and $\text{user}^{\text{lose}}_1$ are the users who lose in this case. Same as, $\text{prov}^{\text{win}}_1$ be the set of providers who successfully get a chance to offer a unit-VM and $\text{prov}^{\text{lose}}_1$ are the users who lose in this case. Let weakest winning user, i.e. $U^{\text{win}}_{\text{weak}}$, is the user with the lowest marginal valuation among winning users and strongest losing user, i.e. $U^{\text{lose}}_{\text{strng}}$, is the user with the highest marginal valuation among the losing users. Similarly, weakest winning provider, i.e. $P^{\text{win}}_{\text{weak}}$, is the provider with the highest marginal valuation among winning providers and strongest losing provider, i.e. $P^{\text{lose}}_{\text{strng}}$, is the provider with the lowest marginal valuation among the losing providers. Price ranges are calculated for both winning and losing users in order to hold the truthfulness property using Eqs. (5.1)–(5.4).

A loser-agent price range, i.e. $\text{price}^{\text{loser}}_{\text{range}} = \left[\underline{\text{price}^{\text{loser}}_{\text{range}}}, \overline{\text{price}^{\text{loser}}_{\text{range}}}\right]$
where

$$\underline{\text{price}^{\text{loser}}_{\text{range}}} = \begin{cases} b^{U^{\text{lose}}_{\text{strng}}}_{\text{first}}, & \text{if user}^{\text{lose}}_1 \text{ and prov}^{\text{lose}}_1 \text{ exists} \\ 0, & \text{otherwise} \end{cases} \tag{5.1}$$

and

$$\overline{\text{price}^{\text{loser}}_{\text{range}}} = \begin{cases} p^{P^{\text{lose}}_{\text{strng}}}_{\text{first}}, & \text{if user}^{\text{lose}}_1 \text{ and prov}^{\text{lose}}_1 \text{ exists} \\ 1, & \text{otherwise} \end{cases} \tag{5.2}$$

Similarly a winner-agent price range, i.e. $\text{price}^{\text{win}}_{\text{range}} = \left[\underline{\text{price}^{\text{win}}_{\text{range}}}, \overline{\text{price}^{\text{win}}_{\text{range}}}\right]$
where

$$\underline{price_{range}^{win}} = \left\{ \begin{array}{ll} P_{first}^{\overline{win}_{strng}}, & \text{if } user_1^{win} \text{ and } prov_1^{win} \text{ exists} \\ 0, & \text{otherwise} \end{array} \right\} \qquad (5.3)$$

$$\overline{price_{range}^{loser}} = \left\{ \begin{array}{ll} b_{first}^{\overline{win}_{strng}}, & \text{if } user_1^{win} \text{ and } prov_1^{win} \text{ exists} \\ 1, & \text{otherwise} \end{array} \right\} \qquad (5.4)$$

A primary reserve price, i.e. $Reserve_{primary}^{price}$, is a function of valuations and costs for the first unit of the losing agents which takes values in loser-agent price range; i.e., primary reserve price does not depend upon the winning agents' values. A Cloud market auctioneer/broker can utilize the statistical information behind the submitted bids and accordingly choose the optimal $Reserve_{primary}^{price}$. The above mechanism reduces to McAfee auction in unit-demand and unit-supply case. In case of McAfee's auction [108] where unit-demand environment and unit-supply environment are considered, $Reserve_{primary}^{price}$ can be calculated as given in Eq. (5.5).

$$Reserve_{primary}^{price} = \frac{\left(price_{range}^{win} + \overline{price_{range}^{win}} \right)}{2} \qquad (5.5)$$

Then, reserve price for both the user and the provider is calculated accordingly as given in Eqs. (5.6) and (5.7), respectively.

$$Reserve_{user}^{price} = \left\{ \begin{array}{ll} Reserve_{primary}^{price}, & \text{if } Reserve_{primary}^{price} \in price_{range}^{win} \\ \overline{price_{range}^{loser}}, & \text{otherwise} \end{array} \right\} \qquad (5.6)$$

And

$$Reserve_{prov}^{price} = \left\{ \begin{array}{ll} Reserve_{primary}^{price}, & \text{if } Reserve_{primary}^{price} \in price_{range}^{win} \\ \underline{price_{range}^{win}}, & \text{otherwise} \end{array} \right\} \qquad (5.7)$$

Total Traded Quantity

Only those buyers who bid above their reserve prices, i.e. $b_1^i > Reserve_{user}^{price}$ are allowed to trade in multi-unit double auction. Similarly, providers with $p_1^j <$ $Reserve_{prov}^{price}$ are eligible for providing their resources. If the marginal valuations of a kth unit of user i are greater than $Reserve_{user}^{price}$, i.e. $b_k^i > Reserve_{user}^{price}$, that unit can be added to the total demand. This condition is checked for all the users, and aggregated quantity is obtained by adding all such units. The aggregated requested quantity $Request^{total}$ at $Reserve_{user}^{price}$ can be calculated as follows.

$Request^{total} = 0$
for $i = 1 : N$

```
    for k = 1 : K
         if b_k^i > Reserve_user^price
         Request^total = Request^total + 1;
         end if;
    end for;
end for;
```

In a similar way, the total offered quantity, i.e. offer^{total} at Reserve$_{\text{prov}}^{\text{price}}$ can be obtained as follows.

```
Offer^total = 0
for i = 1 : N
    for k = 1 : K
         if p_k^i < Reserve_prov^price
         Offer^total = Offer^total + 1;
         end if;
    end for;
end for;
```

The quantity traded is the quantity requested or offered at reserve prices Reserve$_{\text{ser}}^{\text{price}}$ and Reserve$_{\text{prov}}^{\text{price}}$. The quantity traded in the VCG auction is given in Eq. (5.8).

$$Q^{\text{traded}} = \min\left(\text{Request}^{\text{total}}, \text{Offer}^{\text{total}}\right) \tag{5.8}$$

Allocation and Pricing Using VCG Auction

For truthful pricing, VCG mechanisms [135] are used in this work. The values calculated, in the above section, i.e. Q^{traded}, Reserve$_{\text{user}}^{\text{price}}$ and Reserve$_{\text{prov}}^{\text{price}}$, are used to further calculate the final allocated quantity among the users and providers in the second-stage VCG auction. After this, truthful prices are calculated for both user and provider.

Users' Allocated Quantity and Prices

Let $b = (b_{(1)}, b_{(2)}, \ldots, b_{(NK)})$ is a vector of length $(N \times K)$ and a permutation of users' valuation vectors $(_1^1, \ldots, b_K^1, \ldots, b_1^N, \ldots, b_K^N)$ such that $b_{(K)} \geq b_{(K+1)}$. Here, Q^{traded} is the total VMs to be allocated and Reserve$_{\text{user}}^{\text{price}}$ is the user's reserve price in VCG auction. Those users who have higher valuations for these VMs and bid above Reserve$_{\text{user}}^{\text{price}}$ will get the VMs. Let $b_{Q^{\text{traded}}} = (b_{(1)}, b_{(2)}, \ldots, b_{(Q^{\text{user}})})$ denote the marginal valuations of winning users of all the allocated units. Here $Q^{\text{user}} = \max\{q : q \leq Q^{\text{traded}} \text{ and } b_{(q)} > \text{Reserve}_{\text{user}}^{\text{price}}\}$ is the total number of VMs allocated to all users. Number of VMs allocated to each user can be calculated as given in Eq. (5.9).

$$Q_{\text{user}}^i = \max\left(r : b_r^i = b_{(k)} \geq b_{(Q^{\text{user}})}\right) \tag{5.9}$$

A users' payment will depend upon the number of VMs allocated and the bid values of other users. For a winning user, payment is calculated using marginal valuations vector b^i and b^{-i} where b^{-i} represents the marginal valuation vectors of all users except user i; i.e., user i is not participating and $b^{-i} = (b_{(1)}^{-i}, b_{(2)}^{-i}, \ldots, b_{(NK-K)}^{-i})$.

If user i wins, the marginal valuation of user i is greater than the valuation of non-winning users, as users are arranged in decreasing order of their marginal valuations. Therefore, when user i is not participating, this results in the winning of one or more users with lower valuations (as users are sorted in deceasing order of their valuations and user i has higher marginal valuation than new winning users) who successfully obtained their requested VMs. Moreover, user i will pay the marginal valuations of new winning users in order to achieve truthfulness. In other words, each user pays the price equal to the loss caused by it to other users which is measured by the marginal valuation of getting the resources by new winning users [186]. The valuation vector is represented in Eq. (5.10).

Let $b_{\text{user}}^{-i} = (b_{(1)}^{-i}, \ldots, b_{(Q^{\text{traded}})}^{-i})$ where

$$b_{(q)}^{-i} = \begin{cases} b_{(q)}^{-i}, & \text{if } b_{(q)}^{-i} \geq \text{Reserve}_{\text{user}}^{\text{price}} \\ \text{Reserve}_{\text{user}}^{\text{price}}, & \text{otherwise} \end{cases} \forall q = [1, \ldots, Q^{\text{user}}] \qquad (5.10)$$

After calculating the marginal valuation vector, with or without user participation, payment vector for each user can be derived as in Eq. (5.11).

$$\text{pay}_i^{\text{user}} = \left(\text{pay}_1^i, \text{pay}_2^i, \ldots, \text{pay}_{Q^{\text{traded}}}^i\right) = \left(b_{(Q^{\text{traded}})}^{-i}, \ldots, b_1^{-i}\right) \qquad (5.11)$$

Providers' Offered Quantity and Prices

Let $p = (p_{(1)}, p_{(2)}, \ldots, p_{(NK)})$ is a vector of length $(N \times K)$ and a permutation of providers' valuation vector is $(p_1^1, \ldots, p_K^1, \ldots, p_1^N, \ldots, p_K^N)$ such that $p_{(K)} \leq p_{(K+1)}$. Here, Q^{traded} is the total VMs to be allocated and $\text{Reserve}_{\text{prov}}^{\text{price}}$ is the provider's reserve price in VCG auction. Those providers who have lower cost/ask price for these VMs and bid below $\text{Reserve}_{\text{prov}}^{\text{price}}$ will get the chance to offer VMs. Let $p_{Q^{\text{traded}}} = \left(b_{(1)}, b_{(2)}, \ldots, b_{(Q^{\text{prov}})}\right)$ denote the marginal costs of winning providers of all the allocated units that they have to provide. Here, $Q^{\text{prov}} = \max\{q : q \leq Q^{\text{traded}} \text{ and } p_{(q)} < \text{Reserve}_{\text{prov}}^{\text{price}}\}$ is the total number of VMs offered by the providers. Number of VMs offered by each provider can be calculated as given in Eq. (5.12).

$$Q_{\text{prov}}^j = \max\left(r : p_r^j = p_{(k)} \leq p_{(Q^{\text{prov}})}\right) \qquad (5.12)$$

The providers' payment will depend upon the number of VMs offered by the winning providers. For a winning provider, total payment is calculated using marginal cost vector p^j and p^{-j}, where p^{-j} represents the marginal cost vectors of all providers except provider j; i.e., provider j is not participating and $b^{-j} = \left(p_{(1)}^{-j}, p_{(2)}^{-j}, \ldots, p_{(NK-K)}^{-j}\right)$.

If provider j wins, the marginal cost of provider j is less than the cost of non-winning provider as providers are arranged in an increasing order of their marginal cost/ask prices. Therefore, when provider j is not participating, this results in the winning of one or more than one providers with higher marginal costs (as providers are arranged in increasing order of their costs and provider j has lower marginal cost than new winning providers) who successfully offer VMs. Moreover, provider j will pay the marginal costs of new winning providers in order to achieve truthfulness and incentive rationality. In other words, each provider gets the payment equal to the loss caused by it to other providers which is measured by the marginal cost of offering the resources by new winning providers. The cost vector is represented in Eq. (5.13).

Let $p_{\text{prov}}^{-j} = (p_{(1)}^{-j}, \ldots, p_{(Q^{\text{traded}})}^{-j})$ where

$$
p_{(q)}^{-j} = \begin{cases} b_{(q)}^{-j}, & \text{if } b_{(q)}^{-j} \leq \text{Reserve}_{\text{prov}}^{\text{price}} \\ \text{Reserve}_{\text{prov}}^{\text{price}}, & \text{otherwise} \end{cases} \Bigg\} \forall q = \left[1, \ldots, Q^{\text{user}}\right] \qquad (5.13)
$$

After calculating the marginal cost vector, with or without provider participation, payment vector for each provider can be derived as in Eq. (5.14).

$$
\text{pay}_j^{\text{prov}} = \left(\text{pay}_1^j, \text{pay}_2^j, \ldots, \text{pay}_{Q^{\text{traded}}}^j\right) = \left(p_{(Q^{\text{traded}})}^{-j}, \ldots, j\right) \qquad (5.14)
$$

The double auction model TDACC is presented in Algorithm 5.1.

Algorithm 1: TDACC

1. **Input**: $b^i = (b_1^i, b_2^i, \ldots, b_K^i) \forall i \in \mathcal{N}$; vector of user's marginal valuation
2. **Input**: $p^j = \left(p_1^j, p_2^j, \ldots, p_K^j\right) \forall j \in \mathcal{N}$; vector of provider's marginal cost/ask price
3. Determine $\text{Reserve}_{\text{user}}^{\text{price}}$ and $\text{Reserve}_{\text{prov}}^{\text{price}}$ using Eqs. (5.1)–(5.7).
4. Calculate total traded number of VMs Q^{traded} using Eq. (5.8).
5. Determine total number of VMs assigned to each winning user Q_{user}^i using Eq. (5.9).
6. Determine truthful payments done by each winning user $\text{pay}_{\text{user}}^i$ using Eqs. (5.10), (5.11).
7. Determine total number of VMs offered by each winning provider Q_{prov}^j using Eq. (5.12).
8. Determine truthful payments received by each winning provider $\text{pay}_{\text{prov}}^j$ using Eqs. (5.13), (5.14).
9. **Output**: Final Allocation and payment output for user and provider Q_{user}^i, $\text{pay}_{\text{user}}^i$, Q_{prov}^j, $\text{pay}_{\text{prov}}^j$.

Auction Properties of TDACC

The auction properties, of the proposed mechanism, are as follows.

Efficiency

The proposed mechanism is not fully efficient as both efficiency and truthfulness cannot be achieved together according to the impossibility theorem stated in [125]. As the focus is on truthfulness, there is always a compromise with the efficiency. This is also true in case of McAfee auction [108] with unit-demand/unit-supply and multi-unit auction with uniform pricing [86]. The proposed mechanism selects most eligible users and providers with higher valuations and lower offering prices and sacrifices least profitable trades to ensure truthfulness.

Budget-Balance

The mechanism, proposed in this work, is weakly budget-balanced; i.e., a nonnegative surplus is generated from the proposed double auction mechanism as the users always pay more than $\text{Reserve}_{user}^{price}$ and providers will always get less than $\text{Reserve}_{prov}^{price}$ and $\text{Reserve}_{user}^{price} > \text{Reserve}_{prov}^{price}$. This surplus can be retained by auctioneer/market broker (who holds the auction) for sustaining and functioning of the Cloud market.

Incentive Compatibility

The proof of incentive compatibility of the proposed mechanism can be inferred from the literature on VCG mechanisms and Vickrey arguments [11, 186].

For Cloud User

Incentive compatibility property ensures that a participant's dominant strategy is to bid its true information (valuation or ask price). To prove this property, first all possible deviations are considered and then, it has to be shown that its utility will be maximum when it bids truthfully. Let $\widehat{b^i}$ and b^i are the quoted and actual marginal valuation vectors, respectively, of ith user. The following holds then.

(a) Cloud user i wins:

    1. If $\widehat{b^i} < b^i$, then there are two cases
       • It still wins. Therefore, there is no change in its utility.
       • It may lose, and in that case, its utility will be zero.
    2. If $\widehat{b^i} > b^i$, then it will always be a winner because its position in list will go upward (users are sorted in decreasing order of their valuations).

(b) Cloud user i loses:

    1. If $\widehat{b^i} < b^i$, then it will still be a loser in the double auction because of bidding lower than actual valuation which further puts it in the lower position in the list (users are sorted in decreasing order of their valuations).
    2. If $\widehat{b^i} > b^i$, then there are two cases

- It may still be the loser and ends up trading no unit of VMs. In that case also, the deviation remains unprofitable and hence no change in its utility.
- It may be the winner, but in that case, it will pay at least $\overline{\text{Reserve}_{\text{user}}^{\text{price}}} \geq \text{Reserve}_{\text{user}}^{\text{price}} \geq b_1^i$, i.e. more than its valuation. Therefore, its utility will be negative and it suffers loss.

The truthfulness for the Cloud provider can also be proved in the same manner as in the Cloud users' case.

Individual Rationality

All winning Cloud users always pay truthful payments for each unit of VMs they obtain which is less than their marginal valuation, and all Cloud providers always get paid more than their marginal costs/ask prices. In case of non-winning, each participant has zero utility. Therefore, the proposed mechanism is individually rational.

5.5   An Illustrative Example

In this section, TDACC is illustrated by an example by considering simple bid values as shown in Table 5.3.

From the given marginal valuations and costs, reservation prices are calculated by considering the valuation/cost of first unit of VM requested/offered by user/provider as discussed in Sect. 5.4.

Reservation Price Calculation

In the above example, the quantity traded in unit-item case, i.e. Q_{unit}, will be 7 and active buyer set, i.e. $\text{user}_1^{\text{win}} = \{2, 3, 1, 4, 5, 6, 7\}$ and weakest active buyer $U_{\text{weak}}^{\text{win}} = \{7\}$. Similarly, active seller set $\text{prov}_1^{\text{win}} = \{1, 2, 3, 4, 5, 6, 7\}$ and weakest active seller $P_{\text{weak}}^{\text{win}} = \{7\}$. Inactive buyer set $\text{prov}_1^{\text{lose}}$ in this case is $\{8, 9, 10\}$ and strongest inactive buyer $U_{\text{strng}}^{\text{lose}}$ is $\{8\}$, whereas inactive seller set $\text{prov}_1^{\text{lose}}$ is $\{8, 9, 10\}$ and strongest inactive seller $P_{\text{strng}}^{\text{lose}}$ is $\{8\}$. From the above values, inactive traders price gap $\text{price}_{\text{range}}^{\text{lose}} = [0.5263; 0.5263]$ and active traders price gap $\text{price}_{\text{range}}^{\text{win}} = [0.4737; 0.5789]$. From these gaps, preliminary reserve price $\text{Reserve}_{\text{primary}}^{\text{price}}$ will be 0.5263; buyer reserve price $\text{Reserve}_{\text{user}}^{\text{price}}$ will be 0.5263, and seller reserve price $\text{Reserve}_{\text{prov}}^{\text{price}}$ will be 0.5263.

VCG Trades and Prices

After calculation of reservation values of both user and provider, total requested and offered quantities by the users and providers are 13 and 15, respectively. Minimum of these two values will be the final allocated quantity, i.e. $Q^{\text{traded}} = 13$. Users' allocated quantity Q_{user}^i and prices pay^{user} are as follows.

$Q_{\text{user}}^i = [2;2;2; 3;1;2;1;0;0;0]$ and

Table 5.3 Example data

Users	Users' marginal valuations				Providers	Providers' marginal ask prices/costs			
1	0.7368	0.5263	0.2105	0.1053	1	0.1053	0.2632	0.3158	0.4211
2	0.8421	0.5789	0.5263	0.1579	2	0.2105	0.3158	0.4737	0.5263
3	0.6842	0.5789	0.4737	0.4211	3	0.2105	0.2632	0.3684	0.5263
4	0.3684	0.2105	0.1579	0.0526	4	0.2632	0.4737	0.5263	0.5789
5	0.3684	0.2632	0.2105	0.0526	5	0.4211	0.5263	0.5789	0.6316
6	0.5263	0.3684	0.2632	0.2105	6	0.4211	0.5789	0.6842	0.7368
7	0.5789	0.5263	0.4211	0.0526	7	0.4737	0.5263	0.6316	0.7895
8	0.4737	0.3158	0.2105	0.1579	8	0.5263	0.5789	0.6316	0.7895
9	0.4737	0.3158	0.2105	0.1579	9	0.5789	0.7368	0.7895	0.8421
10	0.4211	0.2632	0.2105	0.1053	10	0.5789	0.6842	0.8421	0.9474

pay^{user} = {[0.5263, 0.5263]; [0.5263, 0.5263]; [0.5263, 0.5263]; [0.5263, 0.5263, 0.5263]; [0.5263]; [0.5263, 0.5263]; [0.5263]; [0]; [0]; [0]};

Similarly, providers' offered quantity and prices are as follows.

Q^i_{prov} = [4; 3; 3; 2; 1; 0; 0; 0; 0; 0] and
pay^{prov} = {[0.4737, 0.4211, 0.4211, 0.3684]; [0.4211, 0.4211, 0.3684]; [0.4211, 0.4211, 0.4211]; [0.4211 0.3654]; [0.3654], [0], [0], [0], [0], [0]}.

Through this example, it can be observed that only those users whose marginal valuations are above the reserve price are eligible for the next stage (VCG auction). Same applies to those providers whose marginal costs are less than the Reserve$^{price}_{prov}$.

5.6 Issues and Challenges

Although double auction has not been implemented in a real Cloud as of now, there is a strong possibility of its implementation in Cloud computing in future. Same has been discussed in Sect. 5.2. This section discusses some important issues and challenges possible during and after the implementation of the double auction for Cloud resource provisioning.

One of the main hurdles in the implementation of double auction-based allocation mechanisms is the issue of interoperability as discussed before. In double auction scenario, resources are provided to a user by the multiple providers. To design a standard for the resource offering from multiple and heterogeneous providers is a very complex task. In addition, one also has to deal with the switching cost when a user migrates from one to another provider [23].

In this work, a truthful mechanism has been proposed in a multi-unit environment. These mechanisms cannot be extended to other more complex environment, e.g. combinatorial bidding. Computational complexity is an issue while designing the combinatorial double auction mechanisms. A combinatorial double auction is an NP-hard problem [199], and therefore, to find an exact solution is computationally intractable. Although researchers and academicians have applied various meta-heuristics and approximated solutions for the same, the problem needs further attention [61, 73, 74, 159–161, 163]. Most of the above-cited works mainly focus on the allocation part of the problem giving little attention to the pricing phase of the problem. Although some of the above works proposed new and efficient algorithms for allocation, these works cannot be applied in Cloud scenario as the bidding assumptions considered in these do not suit the Cloud scenario. For example, [154] proposed solutions for the winner determination problem by reducing the problem to linear programming (LP) when a subset of combinations of goods is taken. But this assumption does not fit into the Cloud market as a user will pay only if she obtains all the required resources.

QoS management is another issue in double auction-based Cloud market as proper monitoring of QoS is required in an auction-based market. A double auction mechanism is useful if allocation and pricing results are honoured by all the agents. There might be the case that a provider is not to provide the services with the quoted QoS after winning a bid. In that case, auctioneer can initiate legal action against the provider. Another way to stop such behaviour in the market is priority-, reputation- and penalty-based mechanisms which affect the provider directly or indirectly. The ways for reducing the malicious behaviour of providers in the market are addressed recently in [18, 195]. These works mainly focus on the fair and efficient resource allocation in the double auction-based Cloud market. However, designing these mechanisms with all other properties such as truthfulness, budget-balance is very complex and needs further research. Most of the double auction-based models have considered uni-attribute scenario (price as an attribute). However, as discussed earlier, QoS is equally important in Cloud computing. Multi-attribute version of the double auction is considered for handling these situations. Winner determination problem, in this case, becomes more complex as selection of the winners depends upon many factors. Designing truthful mechanisms, in these scenario, requires a good understanding of types of attributes (qualitative or quantitative) and needs to design strategic payment schemes [141]. Availability/reliability, throughput, response time, efficiency, etc., are some examples of attributes which can be used in multi-attribute double auctions. All Cloud QoS attributes with their definitions and examples are listed in [17]. Various attributes (price as well as non-price) have been considered in [18, 194] while provisioning the resources in the Cloud market.

5.7 Summary

This chapter focuses on the double auction-based resource allocation and pricing mechanisms in the Cloud market. The applicability of the double auction in the Cloud has been explicitly discussed. Various mechanism design properties, a double auction-based design should satisfy, are discussed with their relevance and benefits. All the major double auction-based models in Cloud computing have been surveyed and compared in terms of various auction properties to help the researchers to understand their strengths and weakness. A basic framework of double auction is discussed to understand the fundamental steps in designing real implementation of the double auction. The work further proposes a truthful multi-unit double auction model TDACC and gives an idea of how to design a double auction mechanism with desired goal for the Cloud market. Several issues, identified during the literature survey, are discussed along with the future challenges that need to be addressed.

As real implementation of the double action-based models in Cloud computing has not been done till now, a great opportunity lies for the research community (industry as well as academia) to design efficient, sustainable and viable double auction-based Cloud market mechanisms for Cloud resource provisioning. This chapter intends to encourage the researchers to design such mechanisms by resolving various discussed issues.

Chapter 6
Epilogue

Abstract Amazon provides virtual machines using auction called spot instances besides providing virtual machines with on-demand and reserved policy. Spot instances are real implementation of auction in Cloud computing. In this chapter, first a brief description of Amazon spot market is given to make readers understand that whatever they learnt from this book are going to fetch enormous feasible opportunities in research. The chapter briefly recalls key concepts and key learning points, obtained from this book, along with summarization. Auction itself has a rich literature, and it has not been applied only in economics but in areas in Computer Science also. This chapter brings forth various literature related to auction and its application in other fields of Computer Science for further research.

6.1 Amazon Spot Market: Real Implementation of Auction in Cloud

Amazon Elastic Compute Cloud (Amazon EC2) offers VMs using reserved, on-demand and spot pricing policy, but the emphasis here is on spot pricing [12] only, because spot pricing is an implementation of dynamic pricing, specifically, an implementation of auction. In December 2009, Amazon launched spot market in which customer needs to bid to obtain VMs. Static pricing is widely accepted in any market because of its simplicity. Dynamic pricing helps to achieve equilibrium price but is complex in nature as compared to static pricing as discussed in the first chapter. In Cloud spot market, a customer's win cannot be always guaranteed as the resources may not be available. Further, the resources allocated to customers may be taken back by the provider at any time. In the current Cloud market, customers are rational and intelligent. They are ready to take the decision and use their intelligence to their benefits. They know that spot pricing is suitable for time-flexible and interrupt-tolerant applications. It is difficult for the providers to offer the services which involve the decision-making of customers. This is the reason to state that launching of spot market was a bold move by Amazon. Cloud customers not only well accepted this, but it created a glorious history. Customers could save lot of money using spot instances

© The Author(s) 2018

G. Baranwal et al., *Auction Based Resource Provisioning in Cloud Computing*,
SpringerBriefs in Computer Science, https://doi.org/10.1007/978-981-10-8737-0_6

obtained through spot pricing. Amazon has highlighted the positive experiences of reputed customers at the website of spot instance.

Amazon classifies the tasks that can utilize SIs effectively, in four classes: optional task (which can be executed whenever one wishes), delayable task (tasks with deadline), acceleratable task (execution of which can be accelerated if it gets more resources) and large-scale task (which requires large computational power). Basically, all the applications, which can tolerate interruption or flexible with time, can utilize SIs effectively. These applications can be Web crawling, scientific computing, geospatial analysis, big data analysis, financial analysis, etc. Since auction does not guarantee the availability of resources to each participant, Amazon spot instances are most suitable for fault-tolerant applications. Customers need to have some bid-related information so that they have some idea to start the bidding process. For this, Amazon provides history of price of spot instances of the last 90 days [4].

Amazon determines a Spot Price after reviewing all the bids in each round of auction. All the customers, with bid value greater than spot price, win the auction and need to pay the spot price, not the bid value. Amazon charges on hourly basis to utilize the spot instance. Amazon has a collection of unutilized instances defined as the spot pool. If there is more demand for on-demand and reserved instances, Amazon can pre-empt the allocated SIs and take the allocated spot instances back. Further, if the spot price exceeds the bid price, Amazon can take the assigned spot instances back. Customer itself can terminate SIs normally on no further requirement. If customer terminates SI in latest partial hour, customer has to pay for the whole hour. But if Amazon terminates in latest partial hour, customer need not to pay for that partial hour.

Amazon launched SIs to maximize its resource utilization which in turn will increase its revenue. Though Amazon provides spot price history of 90 days, it is still not clear that how Amazon decides the spot price. Few works [40, 150] suggest that spot price is demand- and supply-dependent, while few others [24, 201] claim that it is not based on supply and demand but is not market-driven. Since SIs are based on auction, various researchers suggested that spot pricing can be modelled with different types of auction [114, 174]. Although history of spot pricing can help in the prediction of spot price and several works tried it also [9, 171, 190], Mazzucco et al. [107] and Zhao et al. [212] claim that prediction of spot price is not possible. This is the reason that modelling and prediction of spot pricing are promising research challenges.

According to [104], goals of Amazon are to maximize the utilization of the resources and to prevent the monopoly of customers in the spot market. SIs are cheaper in comparison with on-demand and reserved instances; therefore, it attracts customers and increases the utilization of the resources, while abrupt termination of SIs by Amazon fulfils the second goal. Marathe [104] listed various modifications but defends that practically these modifications are not implementable. We would suggest readers to read this article.

One major drawback of SIs is its being unreliable. But cost-saving nature of spot instances forced professionals and researchers to develop fault-tolerant mechanism to harness the benefits of SIs. Various works are available that use different mechanisms to ensure fault tolerance in the system such as checkpointing [206], checkpointing and migration [205], application-centric checkpointing [81], redundancy and check-pointing [104], adaptive checkpointing [77], checkpointing, migration and duplication [71, 188] and autocorrelation [100]. To explain fault-tolerant mechanisms is out of scope for this book. The open challenges in spot market research are designing of truthful mechanism, modelling of spot market, bidding strategy design, spot pricing prediction, etc. A detailed discussion on spot market, with future research direction, has been provided in [85, 96, 97].

6.2   Intent of the Book

Cloud computing offers its computing resources in the form of the services to its users. The Cloud users need not need to buy the computing resources forever. The users can avail these resources, as per their requirement, for a certain time period, and the users need to pay only for the actual usage. The enormous benefits of the Cloud have resulted in the increase in a rapid pace of both Cloud users and providers. Therefore, Cloud has become a marketplace where business of computing resources is done. Recently, a sharp increase in the number of Cloud service providers and customers has made the Cloud market more competitive. It also has generated new challenges and issues also that need proper attention from the economic point of view.

There are various economic approaches such as auction [18, 20, 86], negotiation [16], distributive justice [22], game-theoretic approach [21]. that might be well applicable in Cloud. This book deals only with auction-based mechanism to handle the resource provisioning challenges in Cloud. A thorough study, of this book, will enable researchers to design auction-based solutions for resource provisioning in Cloud in a mature way. Use of mechanism design in Cloud market with desired objectives will open a new pathway to handle strategic behaviour of participants. Researchers will be able to formulate auction-based resource allocation strategies in different environments.

Though Cloud is a business model of computing, still very little work that applies auction for Cloud resources is available in the literature. One possible reason may be that researchers, working in this area, are not better with both Computer Science and Economics. With this book, researchers from the economics will get a better understanding of the scope of mechanism design in Computer Science. At the same time, Computer Science researchers will be able to acquire a good knowledge about how the methods available in economics may provide feasible solutions to the problem of Computer Science. This book will also encourage inter-discipline research, i.e. will act as a bridge between Computer Science and Economics specifically Cloud computing and auction.

6.3 Conclusion

This book deliberates on why auction-based resource provisioning methods are well suited in Cloud computing. The first chapter provides a brief of Cloud computing along with pricing for Cloud resources which helps to understand the need of auction in Cloud. The second chapter gives a general sense of auction mechanism. Various possible categorizations of auction, available in the literature, are given so that researchers are able to explore auction in various scenarios of Cloud market. Further, various auction properties along with a brief of mechanism design are explained so that an auction designer can understand its feasible expectation in terms of auction properties and using mechanism design can finally achieve its objectives. Chapters 1 and 2 ensure a good preparation to realize the working of auction in Cloud.

Providers like Amazon can offer its resources either using static pricing or can create a market for auctioning of computing resources to offer spare computing resources. This is done with the help of forward auction. Chapter 3 is dedicated to the forward auction. A detailed description of combinatorial forward auction with their relevance and applicability in Cloud is given. A framework along with possible allocation algorithms and pricing schemes for combinatorial forward auction is also given. Open issues related to forward auction in Cloud are listed and explained at the end of the chapter to motivate the researchers for further contribution in forward auction in Cloud.

When Cloud customer needs computing resources, it can either fetch resources from service provider on rental basis or can publish a proposal in the market. Later one is called reverse auction. After publishing the demand, customer collects offerings of various service providers in the form of bid and then selects a bidder which offers suitable resources at low price. Chapter 4 explains the reverse auction, its benefits and its properties in detail. Further, in this chapter, a framework of reverse auction along with a model for combinatorial reverse auction is provided. This will help the researchers to understand the formulation of the reverse auction in Cloud. Open issues in reverse auction are also listed and explained which will guide the researchers to contribute in this field.

The third type of auction, discussed in this work, is double auction. In this, providers and customers both bid which makes it a resource matching problem. This type of auction is more complex compared to single-sided auction, i.e. forward auction and reverse auction. Chapter 5 is dedicated to double auction. Like Chaps. 3 and 4, this chapter also explains various properties and benefits of the double auction. A framework for the same along with a double auction model is given. This chapter ends with open research issues in double auction.

6.4 To Probe Further

This book is specifically focused on auction-based resource allocation in Cloud computing. It is nearly impossible to provide a comprehensive coverage of auction in general sense. Though the second chapter tries to provide some fundamentals of auction for better readability and understanding, it is not enough for a deeper knowledge. Same is true for Cloud computing. Fortunately, a good literature is available in the form of books and research papers in both the areas, i.e. Cloud computing and auction. This book suggests few related literatures with their importance. The intent is not to confine the readers to these suggestions rather explore and fetch other relevant readings.

Cloud Computing

There are many textbooks that provide good understanding of Cloud computing. We would suggest to go through first four chapters of [33] as these chapters are sufficient for the basic knowledge of Cloud computing. Deeper information on how Cloud computing evolved from distributed computing, cluster computing and grid computing is given in [75]. We would also recommend readers to visit websites of Cloud service providers such as Amazon EC2, Microsoft Azure, Google, RackSpace to know what type of Cloud services they offer. It will give a real feeling to the readers to understand the feasibility of various types of Cloud services.

Game Theory and Mechanism Design

The book entitled "Game Theory and Mechanism Design" by Narahari [128] is a bridge between Engineering Science and Economics. This provides the basics of game theory and mechanism design in a beautiful manner. Few ancient short stories, given in this book, make us realize that game theory and mechanism design are well connected to us from ancient life. Though this book is an extension of the book [127], [127] also provides novel models related to mechanism design in resource procurement in grid computing, sponsored search auction and broadcast protocols for ad hoc networks. These two books are worth if one is interested in interdisciplinary work between Economics and Engineering Sciences. As discussed in the second chapter, mechanism design helps to achieve certain auction properties but requires basic knowledge of game theory. After going through the above-mentioned two books, one can understand game theory and mechanism design and their applications for real-world problems. Some more works presented in [26, 60, 70, 134, 170] are also good to read towards an understanding of algorithmic game theory, algorithmic mechanism design, etc.

Auction in General Sense

Specifically, for auction, "Auction Theory" by Krishna [83] and "Putting Auction Theory to Work" by Milgrom [115] are very good books to read. Internet is very helpful in exploration to enhance our knowledge and a good literature of auction is available over the Internet. For combinatorial auction, one can refer [50]. Winner determination problem in combinatorial auctions is a major problem, and the material available in [93] is helpful to understand that how approximation algorithm is beneficial in the combinatorial auction.

Auction in Computer Science

Proper guidance to computer scientist on why their contributions are required in auction has been provided in [139]. One famous application of auction in Computer Science is spectrum allocation. Three books [41, 101, 204] are good source for auction-based spectrum allocation in wireless communication. After going through these books, one can realize that auction is not confined only to economics.

Non-price Attributes in Multi-attribute Auction

In reverse and double auctions, non-price attributes also take active participation in the winner determination. Consideration of non-price attributes makes auction more complex. A general model for multi-attribute reverse auction has been formulated in [141]. The models for double auction and reverse auction are proposed in [18] and [20], respectively, considering the non-price attributes. Readers can understand various non-price attributes relevant to Cloud computing from [17, 63].

Forward Auction in Cloud Computing

Authors in [209] proposed a model for combinatorial forward auction in Cloud computing and then extended the same work in succession. Few other works are available in [106, 131, 208]. These works help to develop a skill on how new challenges can be identified and solutions can be proposed therefor.

Double Auction in Cloud Computing

Few initial works on double auction in Cloud computing are given in [95, 167]. In [158], not only a model for double auction in Cloud computing is proposed, but to implement auction in Cloud computing an extension to the CloudSim (a well-known simulator for Cloud environment) is proposed and named as CloudAuction [49]. Interested readers may refer to [86] for a detailed study of double auction mechanisms in Cloud computing.

Reverse Auction in Cloud Computing

Manoochehri [103] and Schoenherr [165] are quite interesting texts being helpful in understanding the applicability of reverse auction in general. Specifically, for Cloud, works in [20, 146, 147] are quite good.

6.5 Final Remarks

The Cloud business, that involves various kinds of services, needs economic-based resource allocation methods to increase the resource utilization. Resources are available in the data centre normally in the form of virtual machines, i.e. virtual computing resources. Better resource utilization is not only beneficial for the providers in increasing their revenue but is also an environment-friendly step as the total number of servers will decrease. Pricing of resources is an important factor to motivate the Cloud providers and attract the Cloud customers. In the nascent age of Cloud, providers offered the resources using static pricing because of its simplicity. But with the evolution of the Cloud, competition in the Cloud market has increased and both the participants, i.e. provider and customer, act strategically and are rational. This forced the provider to adopt dynamic pricing. Auction is an implementation of dynamic pricing and is used to decide the value of the resources in the Cloud market. It is a tough decision to make as the seller and buyer both are rational and non-cooperative. The Cloud market is also of the same nature; however, compared to the resources in a general market, attributes of computing resources are different. This book provides a detailed description of auction and various models of auction specifically designed for the provisioning of the computing resources in Cloud computing. We sincerely hope that this book is able to inspire and motivate the researchers. This also expects for further contribution and development in auction-based resource provisioning in Cloud computing.

References

1. Abdelmaboud, A., et al.: Quality of service approaches in cloud computing: A systematic mapping study. J. Syst. Softw. **101**, 159–179 (2015)
2. Abrache, J., et al.: Combinatorial auctions. Ann. Oper. Res. **153**(1), 131–164 (2007)
3. Accenture, W.E.E.: Cloud Computing Can Cut Carbon Emissions by 30–90% (2010)
4. Amazon: Amazon EC2 API Tools: Developer Tools: Amazon Web Services, http://aws.amazon.com/developertools/351
5. Amazon: EC2 Instances Info, http://www.ec2instances.info/
6. Anandalingam, G., et al.: The landscape of electronic market design. Manage. Sci. **51**(3), 316–327 (2005)
7. Anisetti, M., et al.: E-auctions for multi-cloud service provisioning. Proc. IEEE Int. Conf. Serv. Comput. SCC 2014. Section II, 35–42 (2014)
8. Archer, A., Tardos, E.: Truthful mechanisms for one-parameter agents. Proc. IEEE Int. Conf. Clust. Comput. 482–491 (2001)
9. Arevalos, S., et al.: A comparative evaluation of algorithms for auction-based cloud pricing prediction. In: Proceedings—2016 IEEE International Conference on Cloud Engineering, IC2E 2016: Co-located with the 1st IEEE International Conference on Internet-of-Things Design and Implementation, IoTDI 2016. pp. 99–108 (2016)
10. Armbrust, M., et al.: A view of cloud computing. Commun. ACM. **53**(4), 50 (2010)
11. Ausubel, L.M., Cramton, P.: Vickrey auctions with reserve pricing. Econ. Theory. **23**(3), 493 (2004).
12. AWS: Amazon EC2 Spot Instances, https://aws.amazon.com/ec2/spot/
13. Babaioff, M., et al.: On the approximability of combinatorial exchange problems. In: Lecture Notes in Computer Science (including subseries Lecture Notes in Artificial Intelligence and Lecture Notes in Bioinformatics), pp. 83–94. Springer (2008)
14. Bailey, M.: Opportunities in private cloud computing via a turnkey approach. Microsoft White Pap. 1–6 (2011)
15. Ball, M.O., et al.: Auctions for the safe, efficient, and equitable allocation of airspace system resources. Comb. Auction. 507–538 (2010)
16. Baranwal, G., et al.: A negotiation based dynamic pricing heuristic in cloud computing. Int. J. Grid Util. Comput. (2017)
17. Baranwal, G., Vidyarthi, D.P.: A cloud service selection model using improved ranked voting method. Concurr. Comput. Pract. Exp. **28**(13), 685–701 (2016)
18. Baranwal, G., Vidyarthi, D.P.: A fair multi-attribute combinatorial double auction model for resource allocation in cloud computing. J. Syst. Softw. **108**, 60–75 (2015)

© The Author(s) 2018
G. Baranwal et al., *Auction Based Resource Provisioning in Cloud Computing*,
SpringerBriefs in Computer Science, https://doi.org/10.1007/978-981-10-8737-0

19. Baranwal, G., Vidyarthi, D.P.: A framework for selection of best cloud service provider using ranked voting method. In: Souvenir of the 2014 IEEE International Advance Computing Conference, IACC 2014, pp. 831–837 (2014)
20. Baranwal, G., Vidyarthi, D.P.: A truthful and fair multi-attribute combinatorial reverse auction for resource procurement in cloud computing. IEEE Trans. Serv. Comput. 1–1 (2016)
21. Baranwal, G., Vidyarthi, D.P.: Admission control in cloud computing using game theory. J. Supercomput. 72(1), 317–346 (2016)
22. Baranwal, G., Vidyarthi, D.P.: An econometric based model for resource scarcity problem in Cloud computing. In: IEEE CONECCT 2014—2014 IEEE International Conference on Electronics, Computing and Communication Technologies (2014)
23. Beall, S., et al.: The role of reverse auctions in strategic sourcing. CAPS Res. 1–86 (2003)
24. Ben-Yehuda, O.A., et al.: Deconstructing Amazon EC2 spot instance pricing. Proc. 2011 3rd IEEE Int. Conf. Cloud Comput. Technol. Sci. Cloud Com. 1(3), 304–311 (2011)
25. Bernstein, D., et al.: Blueprint for the intercloud—Protocols and formats for cloud computing interoperability. In: Proceedings of the 2009 4th International Conference on Internet and Web Applications and Services, ICIW 2009, pp. 328–336 (2009)
26. Blume, L., et al.: Introduction to computer science and economic theory. J. Econ. Theory. 156, 1–13 (2015)
27. Bonacquisto, P., et al.: A procurement auction market to trade residual cloud computing capacity. IEEE Trans. Cloud Comput. 3(3), 345–357 (2015)
28. Bourne, R.A., Zaidi, R.: A quote-driven automated market. In: Proceedings of AISB Symposium on Information Agents for E-Commerce. AISB (2001)
29. Bratton, K., et al.: Competitive market institutions: double auctions versus sealed bid-offer auctions. Am. Econ. Rev. 72(1), 58–77 (1982)
30. Briest, P., et al.: Approximation techniques for utilitarian mechanism design. Stoc. 40(6), 1587–1622 (2011)
31. Bulow, J., Klemperer, P.: Prices and the winner's curse. RAND J. Econ. 33(1), 1–21 (2002)
32. Buyya, R., et al.: Cloud computing and emerging IT platforms: vision, hype, and reality for delivering computing as the 5th utility. Futur. Gener. Comput. Syst. 25(6), 17 (2009)
33. Buyya, R., et al.: Mastering cloud computing: foundations and applications programming, 1st edn. (2013)
34. Calheiros, R.N., et al.: CloudSim: a toolkit for modelling and simulation of cloud computing environments and evaluation of resource provisioning algorithms. Softw. Pract. Exp. 41(1), 23–50 (2011)
35. Carter, C.R., et al.: Reverse auctions–grounded theory from the buyer and supplier perspective. Transp. Res. Part E Logist. Transp. Rev. 40(3), 229–254 (2004)
36. Cason, T.N., Friedman, D.: Price formation in double auction markets. J. Econ. Dyn. Control. 20(8), 1307–1337 (1996)
37. CATS: Combinatorial auction test suite (CATS), http://www.cs.ubc.ca/ ~ kevinlb/CATS/
38. Chaisiri, S., et al.: Optimization of resource provisioning cost in cloud computing. IEEE Trans. Serv. Comput. 5(2), 164–177 (2012)
39. Chakraborty, I., Kosmopoulou, G.: Auctions with shill bidding. Econ. Theory. 24(2), 271–287 (2004)
40. Chen, J., et al.: Tradeoffs between profit and customer satisfaction for service provisioning in the cloud. Proc. 20th Int. Symp. High Perform. Distrib. Comput. HPDC ' 11, 229 (2011)
41. Chen, Y., Zhang, Q.: Dynamic spectrum auction in wireless communication
42. Chevaleyre, Y., et al.: Issues in multiagent resource allocation (2006)
43. Chichin, S., et al.: Double-sided market mechanism for trading cloud resources. In: 2015 IEEE/WIC/ACM International Conference on Web Intelligence and Intelligent Agent Technology (WI-IAT), pp. 198–205 IEEE (2015)

44. Chichin, S., et al.: Towards efficient greedy allocation schemes for double-sided cloud markets. In: Proceedings—2015 IEEE International Conference on Services Computing, SCC 2015, pp. 194–201 (2015)
45. Clarke, E.H.: Multipart pricing of public goods. Public Choice. **11**(1), 17–33 (1971)
46. Cloud4SOA: Cloud4SOA, http://www.cloud4soa.com/
47. CloudHarmony: ECU, http://blog.cloudharmony.com/2010/05/what-is-ecu-cpu-benchmarking-in-cloud.html
48. Cloudorado: Cloudorado, https://www.cloudorado.com/
49. CloudSim: CloudAuction, www.cloudbus.org/cloudsim/
50. Cramton, P., et al.: Combinatorial auctions. MIT Press, p. 1179 (2006)
51. Daniel, T.E.: Pitfalls in the theory of fairness-comment. J. Econ. Theor. **19**(2), 561–564 (1978)
52. Dillon, T., et al.: Cloud computing: issues and challenges. In: 24th IEEE International Conference on Advanced Information Networking and Applications, pp. 27–33 (2010)
53. Ding, L., et al.: An on-line auction method for resource allocation in computational grids. J. Chem. Pharm. Res. **5**(9), 241–247 (2013)
54. Emiliani, M.L.: Business-to-business online auctions: key issues for purchasing process improvement. Supply Chain Manag. An Int. J. **5**(4), 176–186 (2000)
55. Endriss, U., et al.: Negotiating socially optimal allocations of resources. J. Artif. Intell. Res. **25**, 315–348 (2006)
56. Engelbrecht-Wiggans, R.: On optimal reservation prices in auctions. Manage. Sci. **33**(6), 763–770 (1987)
57. Farajian, N., Zamanifar, K.: Market-Driven Continuous Double Auction Method for Service Allocation in Cloud Computing. Presented at the (2013)
58. Fard, H.M., et al.: A truthful dynamic workflow scheduling mechanism for commercial multicloud environments. IEEE Trans. Parallel Distrib. Syst. **24**(6), 1203–1212 (2013)
59. Friedman, D.: The double auction market institution: a survey. Double Auction Mark. Inst. Theor. Evid. **14**, 3–25 (1993)
60. Fu, H., et al.: Algorithmic game theory. Algorithmic Game Theor. Lect. Notes Comput. Sci. 168–179 (2012)
61. Fujishima, Y., et al.: Taming the computational complexity of combinatorial auctions: Optimal and approximate approaches. IJCAI Int. Jt. Conf. Artif. Intell. **1**, 548–553 (1999)
62. Fujiwara, I., et al.: Applying double-sided combinatorial auctions to resource allocation in cloud computing. In: Proceedings—2010 10th Annual International Symposium on Applications and the Internet, SAINT 2010, pp. 7–14 (2010)
63. Garg, S.K., et al.: A framework for ranking of cloud computing services. Futur. Gener. Comput. Syst. **29**(4), 1012–1023 (2013)
64. Ghosh, A., Roth, A.: Selling privacy at auction. Games Econ. Behav. **91**, 334–346 (2015)
65. Giovannucci, A., et al.: iBundler: an agent-based decision support service for combinatorial negotiations. In: AAAI, pp. 1012–1013 (2004)
66. Google: Google cluster data, http://code.google.com/p/googleclusterdata/
67. Groves, T.: Incentives in teams. Econometrica **41**(4), 617–631 (1973)
68. Grozev, N., Buyya, R.: Inter-cloud architectures and application brokering: taxonomy and survey. Softw. Pract. Exp. **44**(3), 369–390 (2014)
69. Gruyer, N., Lenoir, N.: Auctioning airport slots (?) (2003).
70. Halpern, J.Y.: A computer scientist looks at game theory. Games Econ. Behav. **45**(1), 114–131 (2003)
71. He, X., et al.: Cutting the cost of hosting online services using cloud spot markets. In: Proceedings of the 24th International Symposium on High-Performance Parallel and Distributed Computing—HPDC'15, pp. 207–218. ACM Press, New York, USA (2015)
72. Hohner, G., et al.: Combinatorial and quantity-discount procurement auctions benefit mars, incorporated and its suppliers. Interfaces (Prov.) **33**(1), 23–35 (2003)

73. Hoos, H.H., Boutilier, C.: Solving combinatorial auctions using stochastic local search. In: AAAI/IAAI, pp. 22–29 (2000)
74. Hsieh, F.S., Liao, C.S.: An efficient method to find approximate solutions for combinatorial double auctions. In: 2013 10th International Conference on Service Systems and Service Management - Proceedings of ICSSSM 2013, pp. 698–703 (2013)
75. Hwang, K., et al.: Distributed and cloud computing: from parallel processing to the Internet of things
76. Izakian, H., et al.: An auction method for resource allocation in computational grids. Futur. Gener. Comput. Syst. **26**(2), 228–235 (2010)
77. Jangjaimon, I., Tzeng, N.-F.: Effective cost reduction for elastic clouds under spot instance pricing through adaptive checkpointing. IEEE Trans. Comput. **64**(2), 1 (2014).
78. Kang, L., Parkes, D.C.: A Decentralized Auction Framework to Promote Efficient Resource Allocation in Open Computational Grids (2007)
79. Kant, U., Grosu, D.: Double auction protocols for resource allocation in grids. Int. Conf. Inf. Technol. Coding Comput. **II**, 1 (2005)
80. Kaplan, T.R., Zamir, S.: Advances in auctions. Handb. Game Theor. Econ. Appl. **4**(1), 381–453 (2015)
81. Khatua, S., Mukherjee, N.: Application-centric resource provisioning for Amazon EC2 spot instances. In: Lecture Notes in Computer Science (including subseries Lecture Notes in Artificial Intelligence and Lecture Notes in Bioinformatics), pp. 267–278. Springer (2013)
82. Khethavath, P., et al.: Introducing a distributed cloud architecture with efficient resource discovery and optimal resource allocation. In: 2013 IEEE Ninth World Congress on Services, pp. 386–392 (2013)
83. Krishna, V.: Auction Theory (2003)
84. Krishna, V., Perry, M.: Efficient mechanism design. Available SSRN 64934. 1995, 1–19 (1998)
85. Kumar, D., et al.: A survey on spot pricing in cloud computing. J. Netw. Syst. Manag. 1–48 (2017)
86. Kumar, D., et al.: A systematic study of double auction mechanisms in cloud computing. J. Syst. Softw. **125**, 234–255 (2017)
87. Kurze, T., et al.: Cloud federation. In: Cloud Computer 2011, Second International Conference on Cloud Computer GRIDs, Virtualization, pp. 32–38 (2011)
88. Lavi, R.: Computationally efficient approximation mechanisms. Algorithmic Game Theor. 301–329 (2007)
89. Lee, C., et al.: A real-time group auction system for efficient allocation of cloud internet applications. IEEE Trans. Serv. Comput. **8**(2), 251–268 (2015)
90. Lee, J.-S.: Recurrent Auctions in E-commerce (2007)
91. Lee, J.S., Szymanski, B.K.: A novel auction mechanism for selling time-sensitive e-services. In: Proceedings of the Seventh IEEE International Conference on E-Commerce Technology CEC 2005, July, pp. 75–83 (2005)
92. Lee, J.S., Szymanski, B.K.: Apparatus and method for conducting a recurring auction using a participant retention mechanism (2014)
93. Lehmann, D., O'Callaghan, L.I.: Truth revelation in approximately efficient combinatorial auctions. J. ACM. **49**(5), 1–35 (2002)
94. Li, H., et al.: Virtual machine trading in a federation of clouds: individual profit and social welfare maximization. IEEE/ACM Trans. Netw. **24**(3), 1827–1840 (2016)
95. Li, L., et al.: Pricing in combinatorial double auction-based grid allocation model. J. China Univ. Posts Telecommun. **16**(3), 59–65 (2009)
96. Li, Z., et al.: On cloud spot market: an overview of the research (2015)
97. Li, Z., et al.: Spot pricing in the cloud ecosystem: a comparative investigation. J. Syst. Softw. **114**, 1–19 (2016)
98. Liang, Z.Y., et al.: Reverse auction-based grid resources allocation. Agent Comput. Multi-Agent Syst. **4088**, 150–161 (2006)

99. Likhodedov, A. et al.: Mechanism for optimally trading off revenue and efficiency in multi-unit auctions. Agent-Mediated Electron. Commer. V Des. Mech. Syst. 3048, 92–108 (2004)
100. Lim, S.H., et al.: Analyzing reliability of virtual machine instances with dynamic pricing in the public cloud. In: Proceedings of the International Parallel and Distributed Processing Symposium, IPDPS, pp. 885–893 (2014)
101. Lin, P., et al.: Auction Design for the Wireless Spectrum Market, Springer (2014)
102. Mabert, V.A., Skeels, J.A.: Internet reverse auctions: valuable tool in experienced hands. Bus. Horiz. 45(4), 70–76 (2002)
103. Manoochehri, G., Lindsy, C.: Reverse auctions: benefits, challenges, and best practices. Calif. J. Oper. Manag. 6(1), 123–130 (2008)
104. Marathe, A., et al.: Exploiting redundancy and application scalability for cost-effective, time-constrained execution of HPC applications on amazon EC2. In: IEEE Transactions on Parallel and Distributed Systems, pp. 1–1 (2015)
105. Mas-Colell, A., et al.: Microeconomic Theory (1995)
106. Mashayekhy, L., et al.: A PTAS mechanism for provisioning and allocation of heterogeneous cloud resources. IEEE Trans. Parallel Distrib. Syst. 26(9), 2386–2399 (2015)
107. Mazzucco, M., Dumas, M.: Achieving performance and availability guarantees with spot instances. In: Proceedings of the 2011 IEEE International Conference on HPCC 2011—2011 IEEE International Workshop on FTDCS 2011—Workshops of the 2011 International Conference on UIC 2011—Workshops of the 2011 International Conference on ATC 2011, pp. 296–303 (2011)
108. McAfee, R.P.: A dominant strategy double auction. J. Econ. Theor. 56(2), 434–450 (1992)
109. McAfee, R.P.: Auction design for personal communications services. PacTel Exhib. PP Docket. 93–253 (1993)
110. Mell, P., Grance, T.: The NIST definition of cloud computing recommendations of the national institute of standards and technology. Nist Spec. Publ. 145, 7 (2011)
111. Menezes, F.M., Monteiro, P.K.: An Introduction to Auction Theory. Oxford University Press (2005)
112. Microsoft: Microsoft Azure, https://azure.microsoft.com/en-in/
113. Mihailescu, M., Teo, Y.M.: Dynamic resource pricing on federated clouds. In: CCGrid 2010—10th IEEE/ACM International Conference on Cluster, Cloud, and Grid Computing, pp. 513–517 (2010)
114. Mihailescu, M., Teo, Y.M.: The impact of user rationality in federated clouds. In: 2012 12th IEEE/ACM International Symposium on Cluster, Cloud and Grid Computing (ccgrid 2012), pp. 620–627. IEEE (2012)
115. Milgrom, P.: Putting auction theory to work. Cambridge University Press, Cambridge (2004)
116. Milgrom, P.R.: Putting auction theory to work: the simultaneous ascending auction. J. Polit. Econ. 108(2), 245 (2000)
117. Miller, H.P.: Motivation and personality development. Am. J. Occup. Ther. Off. Publ. Am. Occup. Ther. Assoc. 10(6), 62–27(1956).
118. Mochón, A., Sáez, Y.: Understanding auctions. Springer International Publishing, Cham (2015)
119. ModaClouds: ModaClouds, http://www.modaclouds.eu/
120. Di Modica, G., et al.: Procurement auctions to trade computing capacity in the cloud. In: Proceedings—2013 8th International Conference on P2P, Parallel, Grid, Cloud and Internet Computing, 3PGCIC 2013, pp. 298–305 (2013)
121. Müller, J.P., et al.: Multiagent system technologies. In: Multiagent System Technologies—6th German Conference, pp. 147–158 (2015)
122. Murillo, J., et al.: Fairness in recurrent auctions with competing markets and supply fluctuations. Comput. Intell. 28(1), 24–50 (2012)

123. Murillo, J., et al.: Schedule coordination through egalitarian recurrent multi-unit combinatorial auctions. Appl. Intell. **34**(1), 47–63 (2011)
124. Myerson, R.B.: Optimal auction design. Math. Oper. Res. **6**(1), 58–73 (1981)
125. Myerson, R.B., Satterthwaite, M.A.: Efficient mechanisms for bilateral trading. J. Econ. Theor. **29**(2), 265–281 (1983)
126. Naik, A.K., Baranwal, G.: Allocation of Resource Using Penny Auction in Cloud Computing. Presented at the (2018)
127. Narahari, Y.; Garg, D.; Narayanam, R.; Prakash, H.: Game Theoretic Problems in Network Economics and Mechanism Design Solutions, pp. 1–274. Springer (2009)
128. Narahari, Y.: Game Theory and Mechanism Design. World Scientific (2014)
129. Nash, P.G.: Introducing Preemptible VMs, a New Class of Compute Available at 70% Off Standard Pricing
130. Nassiri-Mofakham, F., et al.: Bidding strategy for agents in multi-attribute combinatorial double auction. Expert Syst. Appl. **42**(6), 3268–3295 (2015)
131. Nejad, M.M., et al.: A family of truthful greedy mechanisms for dynamic virtual machine provisioning and allocation in clouds.pdf. IEEE Trans. Parallel Distrib. Syst. **26**(2), 594–603 (2015)
132. Nejad, M.M., et al.: Truthful greedy mechanisms for dynamic virtual machine provisioning and allocation in clouds. IEEE Trans. Parallel Distrib. Syst. **26**(2), 594–603 (2015)
133. Nisan, N.: Algorithmic Game Theory (2007)
134. Nisan, N., Ronen, A.: Algorithmic mechanism design. Games Econ. Behav. **35**(1–2), 166–196 (2001)
135. Nisan, N., Ronen, A.: Computationally feasible VCG mechanisms. J. Artif. Intell. Res. **29**, 19–47 (2007)
136. Osborne, M.J.: A Course in Game Theory (1995)
137. Pardo, J., Flavin, A., Rose, M.: 2015 Top Markets Report—Cloud Computing (2015)
138. Parkes, D.C., et al.: Achieving budget-balance with Vickrey-based payment schemes in exchanges. In: IJCAI International Joint Conference on Artificial Intelligence, pp. 1161–1168 (2001)
139. Parsons, S., et al.: Auctions and bidding. ACM Comput. Surv. **43**(2), 1–59 (2011)
140. Petcu, D.: Multi-cloud: expectations and current approaches. Proc. 2013 Int. Work. Multi-cloud Appl. Fed. clouds MultiCloud '13 **1** (2013)
141. Pla, A., et al.: Multi-attribute auctions with different types of attributes: enacting properties in multi-attribute auctions. Expert Syst. Appl. **41**(10), 4829–4843 (2014)
142. Pla, A., et al.: Multi-dimensional fairness for auction-based resource allocation. Knowledge-Based Syst. **73**, 134–148 (2015)
143. Pla Planas, A.: Multi-attribute Auctions: Application to Workflow Management Systems (2014)
144. Plott, C.R.: The multiple unit double auction. J. Econ. Behav. Organ. **13**(2), 245–258 (1990)
145. Poole, C.M., et al.: Technical Note: Radiotherapy dose calculations using GEANT4 and the Amazon Elastic Compute Cloud, http://arxiv.org/abs/1105.1408
146. Prasad, A.S., Rao, S.: A mechanism design approach to resource procurement in cloud computing. IEEE Trans. Comput. **63**(1), 17–30 (2014)
147. Prasad G,V., et al.: A combinatorial auction mechanism for multiple resource procurement in cloud computing. In: International Conference on Intelligent Systems Design and Applications, ISDA, pp. 337–344 (2012)
148. Prodan, R., et al.: Double auction-based scheduling of scientific applications in distributed grid and cloud environments. J. Grid Comput. **9**(4), 531–548 (2011)
149. Qian, X., et al.: An improved particle swarm optimization algorithm for winner determination in multi-attribute combinatorial reverse auction. In: Proceedings of the 2014 11th World Congress on Intelligent Control and Automation (WCICA), pp. 605–609 (2014)

150. Qi, Z., et al.: Dynamic resource allocation for spot markets in cloud computing environments. In: 2011 Fourth IEEE International Conference on Utility and Cloud Computing, pp. 178–185 (2011)

151. Rassenti, S.J., et al.: A combinatorial auction mechanism for airport time slot allocation. Bell J. Econ. **13**(2), 402–417 (1982)

152. REMICS: REMICS, http://www.remics.eu/

153. Reyes-Moro, A., Rodriguez-Aguilar, J.A.: iAuctionMaker: a decision support tool for mixed bundling. In: Agent-Mediated Electronic Commerce Vi: Theories for and Engineering of Distributed Mechanisms and Systems, pp. 202–214 Springer (2005)

154. Rothkopf, M.H., et al.: Computationally manageable combinational auctions. Manage. Sci. **44**(8), 1131–1147 (1998)

155. Rothkopf, M.H.: Thirteen reasons why the Vickrey-Clarke-groves process is not practical. Oper. Res. **55**(2), 191–197 (2007)

156. Sabzevari, R.A.: Double combinatorial auction based resource allocation in cloud computing by combinational using of ICA and genetic algorithms. Int. J. Comput. Appl. **110**(12), 8887 (2015)

157. Sajid, M., Raza, Z.: Cloud computing: issues and challenges. In: International Conference on Cloud, Big Data and …, pp. 34–41 (2013)

158. Samimi, P., et al.: A combinatorial double auction resource allocation model in cloud computing. Inf. Sci. (Ny) **357**, 201–216 (2016)

159. Sandholm, T.: Algorithm for optimal winner determination in combinatorial auctions. Artif. Intell. **135**(1–2), 1–54 (2002)

160. Sandholm, T.: An algorithm for optimal winner determination in combinatorial auctions. In: IJCAI International Joint Conference on Artificial Intelligence, pp. 542–547 (1999)

161. Sandholm, T., et al.: CABOB: a fast optimal algorithm for combinatorial auctions. IJCAI Int. Jt. Conf. Artif. Intell. **51**(3), 1102–1108 (2001)

162. Sandholm, T., et al.: CABOB: a fast optimal algorithm for winner determination in combinatorial auctions. Manage. Sci. **51**(3), 374–390 (2005)

163. Sandholm, T., Suri, S.: BOB: improved winner determination in combinatorial auctions and generalizations. Artif. Intell. **145**(1–2), 33–58 (2003)

164. Sawyer, R.L., et al.: Utilities and the issue of fairness in a decision theoretic model for selection. J. Educ. Meas. **13**(1), 59–76 (1976)

165. Schoenherr, T., Mabert, V.A.: Online reverse auctions: common myths versus evolving reality. Bus. Horiz. **50**(5), 373–384 (2007)

166. Schubert, L., et al.: The future of cloud computing. opportunities for european cloud computing beyond 2010. Eur. Comm. Cloud Expert Gr. 66 (2010)

167. Shang, S., et al.: DABGPM: a double auction bayesian game-based pricing model in cloud market. In: Lecture Notes in Computer Science (Including Subseries Lecture Notes in Artificial Intelligence and Lecture Notes in Bioinformatics), pp. 155–164 (2010)

168. Sharma, U., et al.: Kingfisher: cost-aware elasticity in the cloud. In: Proceedings—IEEE INFOCOM, pp. 206–210 (2011)

169. Shi, H., et al.: Fairness in wireless networks: issues, measures and challenges. IEEE Commun. Surv. Tutorials **16**(1), 5–24 (2014)

170. Shoham, Y., Leyton-brown, K.: Multiagent systems: algorithmic, game-theoretic, and logical foundations. Revision **54**, 1–4, 513 (2009)

171. Singh, V.K., Dutta, K.: Dynamic price prediction for amazon spot instances. In: Proceedings of the Annual Hawaii International Conference on System Sciences, pp. 1513–1520. IEEE (2015)

172. Snaith, B., et al.: Emergency ultrasound in the prehospital setting: the impact of environment on examination outcomes. Emerg. Med. J. **28**(12), 1063–1065 (2011)

173. Song, B., et al.: A novel cloud market infrastructure for trading service. Proc. 2009 Int. Conf. Comput. Sci. Its Appl. ICCSA, 44–50 (2009)

174. Song, K., et al.: Improving the revenue, efficiency and reliability in data centre spot market: A truthful mechanism. In: Proceedings—IEEE Computer Society's Annual International Symposium on Modelling, Analysis, and Simulation of Computer and Telecommunications Systems, MASCOTS, pp. 222–231. IEEE (2013)
175. Stary, C.: Dynamic Pricing and Automated Resource Allocation for Complex Information Services. Springer Science & Business Media (2007).
176. Sulistio, A., et al.: Managing cancellations and no-shows of reservations with overbooking to increase resource revenue. Proc. CCGRID 2008—Eighth IEEE International Symposium on Cluster Computing, pp. 267–276 (2008)
177. Sun, J., et al.: An intelligent resource allocation mechanism in the cloud computing environment. In: 2013 IEEE 3rd International Conference on Information Science and Technology, ICIST 2013, pp. 744–750 (2013)
178. Sun, Z., et al.: A combinatorial double auction mechanism for cloud resource group-buying. In: 2014 IEEE 33rd International Performance Computing and Communications Conference, IPCCC 2014, pp. 1–8 (2015)
179. Tan, Z., Gurd, J.R.: Market-based grid resource allocation using a stable continuous double auction. In: Grid Computing 2007 8th IEEE/ACM International Conference, pp. 283–290 (2007)
180. Tclouds-project: Tclouds-project, http://www.tclouds-project.eu/
181. The Royal Swedish Academy of Science: The Prize in Economic Sciences 2007 (2007)
182. Thethi, J.P.: Realizing the Value Proposition of Cloud Computing—CIO 's Enterprise IT Strategy for Cloud—When Should CIOs Consider Leveraging Cloud Computing. Infosys White Paper, pp. 1–9 (2009)
183. Toosi, A.N., et al.: Interconnected cloud computing environments. ACM Comput. Surv. **47** (212), 1–47 (2014)
184. Urgaonkar, B., et al.: Analytic modelling of multitier Internet applications. ACM Trans. Web. **1**(1), 2–es (2007)
185. Varian, H.R.: Economic Mechanism Design for Computerized Agents. Proc. USENIX Work. Electron. Commer. July 11–12. May, 1–14 (1995)
186. Vickrey, W.: Counterspeculation, auctions, and competitive sealed tenders. J. Fin. **16**(1), 8–37 (1961)
187. Vinyals, M., et al.: A test suite for the evaluation of mixed multi-unit combinatorial auctions. J. Algor. **63**(1–3), 130–150 (2008)
188. Voorsluys, W., Buyya, R.: Reliable provisioning of spot instances for compute-intensive applications. In: Proceedings—International Conference on Advanced Information Networking and Applications, AINA, pp. 542–549 (2012)
189. de Vries, S., Vohra, R.V.: Combinatorial auctions: a survey. Informs. J. Comput. **15**(3), 284–309 (2003)
190. Wallace, R.M., et al.: Applications of neural-based spot market prediction for cloud computing. In: Proceedings of the 2013 IEEE 7th International Conference on Intelligent Data Acquisition and Advanced Computing Systems, IDAACS 2013, pp. 710–716 (2013)
191. Wang, L., et al.: A novel resource management scheme for cloud computing. Proc. IEEE Int. Conf. Softw. Eng. Serv. Sci. ICSESS, 876–880 (2014)
192. Wang, Q. et al.: When cloud meets eBay: towards effective pricing for cloud computing. In: Proceedings—IEEE INFOCOM, pp. 936–944 (2012)
193. Wang, X., et al.: An intelligent economic approach for dynamic resource allocation in cloud services. IEEE Trans. Cloud Comput. **3**(3), 275–289 (2015)
194. Wang, X., et al.: Resource allocation in cloud environment: a model based on double multi-attribute auction mechanism. In: 2014 IEEE 6th International Conference on Cloud Computing Technology and Science, pp. 599–604. IEEE (2014)
195. Wang, X.X., et al.: A resource auction based allocation mechanism in the cloud computing environment. In: Parallel and Distributed Processing Symposium Workshops PhD Forum (IPDPSW), 2012 IEEE 26th International, pp. 2111–2115 (2012)

196. Wellman, M.P., et al.: Designing the Market Game for a Trading Agent Competition (2001)
197. Wise, R., Morrison, D.: Beyond the exchange–the future of B2B. Harv. Bus. Rev. **78**(6), 86–96 (2000)
198. Wu, X., et al.: A scalable and automatic mechanism for resource allocation in self-organizing cloud. Peer-to-Peer Netw. Appl. **9**(1), 28–41 (2016)
199. Xia, M., et al.: Solving the combinatorial double auction problem. Eur. J. Oper. Res. **164** (1), 239–251 (2005)
200. Xiao, L., et al.: Incentive-based scheduling for market-like computational grids. IEEE Trans. Parallel Distrib. Syst. **19**(7), 903–913 (2008)
201. Xu, H., Li, B.: Dynamic cloud pricing for revenue maximization. IEEE Trans. Cloud Comput. **1**(2), 158–171 (2013)
202. Xu, H., Yang, B.: An incentive-based heuristic job scheduling algorithm for utility grids. Futur. Gener. Comput. Syst. **49**, 1–7 (2015)
203. Xu, K., et al.: Online combinatorial double auction for mobile cloud computing markets. In: 2014 IEEE 33rd International Performance Computing and Communications Conference (IPCCC), pp. 1–8 (2014)
204. Yi, C., Cai, J.: Market-driven spectrum sharing in cognitive radio. Springer International Publishing, Cham (2016)
205. Yi, S., et al.: Monetary cost-aware checkpointing and migration on amazon cloud spot instances. IEEE Trans. Serv. Comput. **5**(4), 512–524 (2012)
206. Yi, S., et al.: Reducing costs of spot instances via checkpointing in the amazon elastic compute cloud. In: Proceedings—2010 IEEE 3rd International Conference on Cloud Computing, CLOUD 2010, pp. 236–243 (2010)
207. Yu, J., et al.: Multi-objective planning for workflow execution on Grids. Proc. IEEE/ACM Int. Work. Grid Comput. 10–17 (2007)
208. Zaman, S., Grosu, D.: A combinatorial auction-based mechanism for dynamic VM provisioning and allocation in clouds. IEEE Trans. Cloud Comput. **1**(2), 129–141 (2013)
209. Zaman, S., Grosu, D.: Combinatorial auction-based allocation of virtual machine instances in clouds. J. Parallel Distrib. Comput. **73**(4), 495–508 (2013)
210. Zaman, S., Grosu, D.: Efficient bidding for virtual machine instances in clouds. In: Proceedings—2011 IEEE 4th International Conference on Cloud Computing, CLOUD 2011, pp. 41–48 (2011)
211. Zhan, R.L.: Optimality and efficiency in auctions design: a survey. In: Springer Optimization and Its Applications, pp. 437–454 (2008)
212. Zhao, H., et al.: Optimal resource rental planning for elastic applications in cloud market. In: Proceedings of the 2012 IEEE 26th International Parallel and Distributed Processing Symposium, IPDPS 2012, pp. 808–819. IEEE (2012)
213. Zheng, L., et al.: How to bid the cloud. In: ACM Conference on Special Interest Group on Data Communication (SIGCOMM 2015), pp. 71–84 (2015)
214. Zheng, Z., et al.: STAR: strategy-proof double auctions for multi-cloud. Multi-tenant bandwidth reservation. IEEE Trans. Comput. **64**(7), 2071–2083 (2014)

Printed in the United States
By Bookmasters